Mississippi's
Exiled Daughter

MISSISSIPPI'S EXILED DAUGHTER

How My Civil Rights Baptism Under Fire Shaped My Life

BRENDA TRAVIS
WITH JOHN OBEE

Foreword by Bob Moses
Afterword by J. Randall O'Brien

NEWSOUTH BOOKS
Montgomery

NewSouth Books
105 S. Court Street
Montgomery, AL 36104

Publisher's Cataloging-in-Publication data

Travis, Brenda, 1945
Mississippi's exiled daughter: how my civil rights baptism under fire
    shaped my life / Brenda Travis ; foreword by Bob Moses ; afterword by
    J. Randall O'Brien
        p. cm.
    Includes photos, bibliography, index.
    ISBN 978-1-58838-329-7 (trade paper)
    ISBN 978-1-60306-422-4 (ebook)
    1. Travis, Brenda. 2. Civil rights workers—Southern States—
Biography. 3. African Americans—Mississippi—Biography. 4. African
Americans—Civil rights—Mississippi—History—20th century. 5.
African Americans—Civil rights—Southern States—History—20th
century. 6. Civil rights movements—Mississippi—History—20th
century. 7. Civil rights movements—Civil rights—Southern States—
History—20th century. 8. Mississippi—Race relations—History—20th
century. 9. Southern States—Race relations—History—20th century. 10.
Mississippi—Biography. I. Obee, John, 1946– II. Title.
                                                            2017959104

Design by Randall Williams

Printed in the United States of America by Versa

.

BRENDA TRAVIS DEDICATES THIS book . . .

To my deceased loved ones, Grandmother Hattie Houston and my mother and father, Icie and LS Travis; to Sister Bobbye Cooper, Brother Harry Lee Martin, and all the brave ancestors who fought so valiantly during a time that was more difficult than I ever imagined. They were the basis of my strong foundation and how I learned resiliency at an early age.

To Dr. Marionette Travis Dallas—my sister, mentor, best friend, and confidant. I deeply appreciate you. You were always there when I was at many low ebbs and encouraging me to write and share with the world my quest for a better life for myself, family and others. When at the age of sixteen, I answered a call of duty to mankind to change the devastating "Jim Crow" laws in Mississippi, little did I know that you would follow in my footsteps and become one of the first black students to integrate the McComb High School. Your courage helped advance my dream and to pave the way for others to accomplish their dreams.

To Emogene Webb, my next to the eldest sister—thanks always for your encouraging words.

To James Kate, my brother, my prayer partner, my friend. It took courage to remain in Mississippi after your experiences as a young man and military life. It took a true act of bravery to remain there and raise my beautiful nieces and nephews.

To Gloria Travis—my youngest sister, you suffered along with my other siblings but probably more in that our mother was forced to leave you with other family members in order to make provisions for the family. You stayed the course and completed high school in spite of the void and the odds stacked against you.

To all nieces, nephews, and cousins which are too numerous to mention. I love you all.

JOHN OBEE DEDICATES THIS book:

To my wife, Janice, the love of my life, and my daughters, Sarah and Rachel, who have always loved and supported me unconditionally. And to all of the unsung heroes of the civil rights movement, whose names do not appear in the history books, such as Nathan Rubin, who in the 1960s took in "white boys" and "white girls" to work in the civil rights movement in Mississippi and I was privileged to be one of those "white boys."

Contents

A selection of photos begins on page 86.

Foreword

Bob Moses*

Whostrophe hen sit-ins for a "Coke & burger" spread in 1960 like wildfire across the upper South and vaulted black subordination under white supremacy into the national conversation, Ella Baker understood as well as anyone in the nation what was up and made her move. From her unheralded spot as interim executive director of the Southern Christian Leadership Conference (SCLC), she organized the Easter Weekend conference for sit-in leaders, which was held at her alma mater, Shaw University, in Raleigh, North Carolina. This gathering opened up the space for black students at historically black colleges and universities (HBCUs) to own their movement through a new organization, the Student Nonviolent Coordinating Committee, (SNCC, pronounced "Snick").

SNCC's coordinating committee held its first meeting in Atlanta that summer and sent its first chairperson, Marion Barry, to voice its demands at the 1960 Republican and Democratic national conventions. It also laid plans to hold the first South-wide meeting of sit-in insurgents in Atlanta that fall. Ella and Jane Stembridge asked if I would make a tour as a SNCC field representative scouting for evidence of sit-in insurgents in Alabama, Mississippi, and Louisiana. Jane, the young white Southerner who had left Union

Theological Seminary to attend the Shaw Easter conference and went on from it to become SNCC's first secretary, sent letters to NAACP leaders on behalf of Ella and SNCC, then sent me off on a Greyhound bus in the month of August 1960.

Brenda Travis, on her summer break from Burglund High School in McComb, her eyes and mind glued to sit-in news, had no way of knowing that SNCC's scout was heading to Mississippi and, as fate would have it, her way. The Brendas of Mississippi were precisely who SNCC had in its sights.

Nine months later, on May 24, 1961, the Brendas of Mississippi watched as the sit-in movement rode-in, two busloads strong. Escorted by the National Guard, state highway patrols, and county sheriffs, SNCC and CORE (Congress of Racial Equality) Freedom Riders were passengers on Greyhound and Trailways buses, riding-in, into Mississippi. SNCC was heading Brenda's way, but it couldn't have had a clue about the role Brenda, a sixteen-year-old, would play just four months later.

The SNCC scouting trip made contact with Amzie Moore, the head of the NAACP in Cleveland, Mississippi. In October 1960, seven months before the Freedom Rides, Amzie had lumbered his Packard to the Atlanta SNCC meeting to push sit-in insurgents to come to the Mississippi Delta to do voter registration. Amzie, the time-tested warrior, and Chuck McDew, tested this time around, made plans. When the ride-in hit, the Mississippi SNCC voter registration insurgency was hatching, Amzie-style.

Amzie intended to start in the all-black town of Mound Bayou with the priest who was already running voter registration workshops out of his Catholic Parish. But before the ride-in, the Mississippi Diocese transferred Father John LaBauve to the Gulf Coast. With no meeting place, Amzie paused, but then C. C. Bryant, who lived down the dirt road from Brenda and spent Saturdays cutting hair in a barbershop shed on his front lawn, made his move. C. C.

spied SNCC's announcement in *Jet* magazine and sent his fellow NAACP "Race Man" a letter requesting one of those SNCC voter registration workers.

In August 1960, I promised Amzie I would return in one year to work for SNCC on his voter registration plans. I made it back in June 1961 and that July Amzie sent me to C. C.'s house. Thus, SNCC's voter registration insurgency was fated to begin in Mc-Comb, down a dirt road from Brenda's house.

"WELL, I RECKON . . ."

Mississippi blacks had a lot to "reckon" before stepping out on a register-to-vote-courthouse journey. Within two months time, economic retaliation, physical violence, and outright murder were all in play. But SNCC Freedom Riders were also in play. Marion Barry, released from Parchman Prison, came to McComb and persuaded Curtis Hayes and Hollis Watkins to reckon the "direct action" way. They gathered a group of twenty or so young teenagers like Brenda to form the "Pike County NonViolent Direct Action Group," and on August 26, 1961, Hollis and Curtis sat-in at McComb's Woolworth's lunch counter. It looked for awhile like "direct action" and "voter registration" insurgencies would take root and grow. But then Brenda sat-in and was sent to juvenile detention, a move that triggered a walkout by her fellow students at Burglund High and forced SNCC to confront the "Nelson Mandela": jail, no bail.

In retrospect, the Mississippi Theater of the civil rights movement took shape as low-grade guerrilla warfare. The NAACP's Amzie Moores and C. C. Bryants constituted the guerrilla base which harbored the SNCC and CORE field secretaries. This was the base within which insurgents could disappear and then reappear to do an action, the base within which they found emotional, intellectual, and cultural grounding.

But we had to earn the right to access this base. We did this in the most direct way possible—every time we got knocked down we stood back up. Even so, Brenda's arrest sent us into territory for which "get back up" was not an option. There is no immediate "get back up" from "jail, no bail." In retaliation for our direct action, Mississippi locked us up and held the jailhouse keys. In retaliation for our voter registration, Mississippi locked us up, but this time the Civil Rights Division (CRD) of the U.S. Department of Justice held the jailhouse keys.

Brenda's sit-in and the subsequent walkout of her fellow students brought into clear focus the fine distinction between the baby and the bath water: two days versus two years. The voter registration legal corridor along which we crawled was the 1957 Civil Rights Act, the first such national legislation since the end of Reconstruction, though in passing it Republican President Dwight Eisenhower and Democratic Senate Majority Leader Lyndon Johnson had Tuskegee Institute professors, not SNCC insurgents, in mind.

We can always ask of our Constitution: What does it require? What does it permit? What does it forbid? The law did not forbid Mississippi from arresting voter registration workers, nor did it require the CRD to defend them. Mississippi voter registration took place in the sphere of the constitutionally permissible. Mississippi was permitted to lock us up; the CRD was permitted to turn the jailhouse key.

Brenda's sit-in cleared the air. When the dust settled and bail money was wired one day before facing "jail, no bail," Curtis and Hollis were easily persuaded to return to voter registration discipline.

"Well I reckon . . ." was still in cultural play, and white supremacy was still in constitutional play, as SNCC and CORE field secretaries over the next three years explored three dimensions of their earned insurgency: their guerrilla base, their relation to the Justice Department CRD, and finally their relation to the nation. For four years SNCC, CORE, and the Mississippi NAACP mounted an earned insurgency, then called on the entire nation to take a closer look at Mississippi through the eyes of young white college students—maybe the only eyes through which the nation could see itself—who participated in Freedom Summer 1964.

But that is getting ahead of our story.

Welcome to this story, the story of a young high school student who had no idea that C. C. Bryant's home, a stone's throw down a dirt road from her own, would become in her sixteenth year the epicenter of a movement to change the nation, one that would also change her life and her relationship to her state, making her into Brenda Travis, Mississippi's exiled daughter.

* Robert Parris Moses is an educator and an icon of the 1960s civil rights movement, known especially for his work with SNCC on voter education and registration in Mississippi. He is a graduate of Hamilton College and Harvard University. As the founder of the Algebra Project, he has received a MacArthur Fellowship and many other awards.

Acknowledgments

FROM BRENDA TRAVIS:

The journey to complete this book has been long and difficult. I have many to thank for encouraging me to tell my story and helping me with the task. In full gratitude, I would like to acknowledge the following individuals who inspired, energized, nourished, and comforted me and sacrificed themselves to help in my quest to give an account of my life in the civil rights movement.

Mr. C. C. Bryant Sr. served as a constant reminder to the black community of the need for change. He tirelessly and without fail encouraged the community to register to vote. He will always be the spoon that fed and nourished me with courage, and inspired me to take a stand.

I thank the Burglund High School students for their commitment, dedication, energy, support, and sacrifices made to walk out of school in protest of Ike Lewis's and my expulsions.

John Obee agreed to co-write the book with me. His diligence and the time he dedicated to the completion of this book, even in the midst of his other responsibilities, encouraged me to keep moving forward. I would like also to thank his wife, Janice, for sharing him with me during this long process.

I would like to thank my editor, Constance (Connie) Curry. Her patience, guidance, feedback and generosity of spirit are greatly appreciated.

I thank Margaret Kibbee for suggesting "Mississippi's Exiled Daughter" as the title for the book.

I also would like to express my sincere gratitude to another integral participant in this journey, Dr. Robert Parris (Bob) Moses, who responded to the call and without hesitation agreed to write a foreword to my book.

Special gratitude goes to Dr. Randall O'Brien, who has played a vital role in my life since I met him. He presented me with the Bronze Star which he received for bravery during the Vietnam war. I have never received such a generous, valuable, and precious gift from a fellow Mississippian. He also wrote the afterword for this book.

I thank all of my siblings and other members of my extended family. You have been and continue to be my rock and cheering squad in all aspects of my life. You keep me grounded.

An extended gratitude goes to the Mississippi Civil Right Veterans Organization for its role in carrying on and promoting the legacy of the civil rights movement in our state.

To all SNCC activists—especially Martha Noonan and Julian Bond who vigorously encouraged me to write this book—I extend my gratitude for the journey we made together. We heeded the call, and we came a long way, but we know the journey is yet to be completed. Remember, *"We all we got."* Thank you for the tumultuous life we shared.

A special thank you goes to my spiritual sister, Frances Wymes-Crenshaw, who has stood in the balance for more than thirty-five years as a sister, friend, prayer warrior, shoulder to lean on, drier of my tears, and an ear to listen without criticizing or passing judgment. You will always be my "sis." Thank you for all you have done and continue to do.

To Betty and Leonard Kyle, I know you always have my back and are ready and willing to lend a helping hand in any way possible—thank you.

FROM JOHN OBEE

My deepest and most heartfelt thanks go to my co-author, Brenda Travis. This book tells Brenda's story, that of a woman who despite incredible obstacles, including many at the hands of white people, remains a loving and trusting person. She entrusted her story to someone who had written many legal publications but had never undertaken a venture such as this. I am in awe of the faith and trust that she placed in me.

Our next thanks, from both Brenda and me, go to Connie Curry, who was involved in the civil rights movement at its earliest stages and who is the author and editor of important books related to the movement. Connie believed in Brenda's story and worked with us to make my sometimes clumsy writing more artful. She also advocated for us with the publisher to see that this most compelling story would become known to the world.

Thanks also goes to people in my law office, particularly to Karen Sanders, who typed the entire manuscript more than once, navigating her way through my sometimes challenging handwriting; and to Michelle Sikorski, my secretary, and Emily Whitworth, who were invaluable with their typing and computer skills.

Lastly, thanks to my good friend and fellow lawyer Kevin Campbell, who helped me with the research for this book and offered his encouragement throughout its preparation.

Mississippi's Exiled Daughter

TENNESSEE

ARKANSAS

The Delta

Mound
Bayou

Parchman

Cleveland

Money

Itta
Bena

Belzoni

Philadelphia

Raymond

Jackson

Meridian

LOUISIANA

Hinds

ALABAMA

Summit

McComb

Amite

Pike

Tylertown

Liberty

Magnolia

Walthall

MISSISSIPPI

1

The Beginnings

McComb, Mississippi.

For most people the name itself does not evoke fear, violence, or repression in relation to the freedom movement of the 1960s. When we hear the name Birmingham, Alabama, we think of bombings and beatings and fire hoses. Philadelphia, Mississippi means the murders of the three civil rights workers, James Chaney, Michael Schwerner, and Andy Goodman. For Selma, Alabama, we recall the deaths of Jimmie Lee Jackson, Reverend James Reeb, and Viola Liuzzo. McComb, Mississippi, escapes such recognition, but during the civil rights movement there were more bombings in McComb than there ever were in Birmingham. One author referred to McComb as "the church burning capital of the world." Beatings and deaths of those involved or who were thought to be involved in civil rights-related activity occurred frequently in McComb and environs, although Herbert Lee, Louis Allen, Charles Moore, and Henry Dee are names far less known than Chaney, Schwerner, Goodman, or Liuzzo. McComb escaped national remembrance, but for those of us who were born into the civil rights movement there, it had more notoriety than many other cities of greater renown.

It was in McComb, Mississippi, that I was born on March 16, 1945. My name is Brenda Laverne Travis, and I descend from a long line of people born in and around McComb. My father's name

3

was LS Travis. The "L" and "S" were not the initials of his given names; they were his name. When he was born, it was common among colored families, as we were called then, to be given just initials without a given name. My father, like my mother, Icie, was born in the ironically named town of Liberty, Mississippi, which is in Amite County, the county adjacent to Pike County where McComb is located. My father never knew his parents, as both died when he was very young. His grandmother took him in but, she was an elderly lady who could not care for my dad and his two siblings. What to do with three young children?

For my dad, a solution was found. A white family by the name of Williams became aware of my father's plight and offered to take him in as they had a son close in age to my dad. But their kindness had a catch. While they fed and clothed my dad, he had to live, sleep, and eat in the barn. His clothes were hand-me-downs from the white son. For his lodging, food, and hand-me-down clothing, my dad was required to work on the farm and in the fields. My father thus became a "sharecropper" at an early age, although his "share" was a bed in the barn, food, and used clothing. The Williams family chose not to educate my father, and he never learned to read or write.

Thanks to oral history, so important in black families, more is known about my mother's family. I will never forget the story that my grandmother, Hattie Houston, shared with me as it was told to her by her mother (my great-grandmother) about the last time she saw her mother, a slave by the given name of Harriet (my great-great-grandmother). They were enslaved on a plantation in Mississippi, which meant they were not considered people; they were considered property. My great-grandmother watched as her mother was loaded onto a horse-drawn wagon and removed from her life forever. She wept as she and her mother locked eyes and watched each other as long as they could. She was helpless to do anything and was so alone. In that instant, a cruel decision beyond her control had made her a motherless child. Circumstances would later make me also into a motherless child, knowing all too well the emotions of being separated from my loved ones. But of course the terrible legacy of slavery is larger than my family story alone; the breakdown of many black families can be traced directly to America's original sin, and America has still not made reparations for it.

Grandmother Houston never married, but she had five children, three by Frank Martin, including my mom, Icie. Later my grandmother moved with her family to McComb, where she worked as a domestic, often the only work available to a black woman with children but no husband.

I do not know how and when my parents met and married, but they lived in McComb with my grandmother and my three older siblings. The way my father was raised had given him experience at farming, and at some point he decided that he needed to move north to the Mississippi Delta*, to work as a sharecropper, if he was going to have meaningful work and income for his expanding family. He left my three older siblings with Grandmother Houston in McComb and took my mother with him to work as a sharecroppers near Itta Bena or Belzoni on a plantation owned by a man named Moon Mullin (similar to the comic strip character, Moon Mullins, although there was nothing comedic about Mr. Mullin the planter).

Both my parents worked on the plantation, and I was conceived there. Just before my mother was ready to deliver—or, to use the expression then in vogue, to "drop her load"—my father was working in the fields, and my mother was in the shack that the plantation owner provided them. Mr. Mullin approached my father and demanded to know why my mother was not also working in

* alluvial floodplain in northwest Mississippi between the Yazoo and Mississippi rivers.

the fields. He ordered him to get my mother out to work in the fields. My dad protested as much as a black man could protest in 1945, telling Mullin that his wife was about to deliver. Mullin took this response as insolence and told my dad that he was going to the "big house" and get his gun. My dad knew this was a serious threat, as Mullin had a reputation for having murdered a number of his black sharecroppers.

While Mullin was on his way to the big house, my dad ran back to the shack and told my mother that they had to flee for their lives. There was no time to gather their belongings because, if they were still on the plantation when Mullin came back with his gun, my father, like many black men before him, was likely a dead man. My parents rushed back to McComb as quickly as they could travel with my mother about to give birth. My dad dropped my mother off at Grandmother Houston's home, where my three siblings were. And then he fled.

As happened to many black men in the South at that time, my father became a marked man. It made no difference that he was only trying to protect his wife; he had "stood up" to a white plantation owner. His limited act of defiance was a death sentence, and my father knew that he would be hunted. He would need to disappear, as many other black men and women had done in the past. He had to flee and go into exile.

This theme of flight and exile haunted my father, and, like father, like daughter, the same theme of flight and exile was later to haunt me as I took a stand for my own rights and the rights of my people.

My mother gave birth to me in McComb. I was a fatherless child and would remain so well into my adulthood.

2

The Early Years in Baertown

The history of McComb, "the Camellia City of America," is well known, at least the history of white McComb. Founded later than many Mississippi cities of its size, McComb was begun in 1872 by a Yankee capitalist as a repair station for the Illinois Central Railroad. Even today, a museum in McComb commemorates its history as a railroad town.

Much of McComb's prosperity was linked to the railroad. The Illinois Central employed many whites and even some blacks. The latter were almost always hired in laborer positions, but those were well-paying jobs by the standards of the black community. The men fortunate enough to obtain such jobs possessed a degree of independence unknown in the larger black community. They belonged to unions, and their jobs neither rested on the whims nor were at risk from the vindictiveness of local whites. This relative independence allowed some black McComb residents, including C. C. Bryant and Webb Owens, to speak out on civil rights and voter registration issues long before the civil rights movement reached McComb in the early 1960s.

However, while a few local blacks achieved economic independence, the vast majority in McComb were very much like my family—poor and dependent upon whites for their livelihood. Even better-off blacks lived in the town's three segregated black neighborhoods, with names virtually unknown outside of these communities: Burglund, Baertown, and Algiers.

I grew up in Baertown in my grandmother's two-bedroom, five-room house on an unpaved street that now, sixty years after my birth and many years after my exile, bears my name—in my growing up years on that nameless dirt road, no one could have imagined such a thing. We had no street address, as our mail was delivered to R.R. Box 136-B on Highway 51, where black Baertown families had mailboxes.

Our small house was filled with adults and children. There was my mother and grandmother and my six siblings, three born before me and three after. I have many attributes of the middle child. I am, and always have been headstrong, and I would need this for my survival during the challenges that confronted me during the civil rights days and beyond. My older siblings were two girls and a boy, Bobbye, Emogene, and James, and my younger siblings were two girls and a boy, Harry, Marionette, and Gloria. I was told that my father reappeared for a short time, when I was around three years old, and during that time my mother conceived my sister, Marionette. My father then had to disappear again because, even years after his original outspokenness, it was still too dangerous for him in Mississippi. I have no recollection of my dad from this period of time.

Besides the nine of us in our two-bedroom home, there were usually others staying there with us. It was not uncommon, even in very impoverished black families such as mine, to take in other relatives who had to find a place to stay quickly because something catastrophic had happened. Thus, my mother's sister, Aunt Maggie Washington, and her children were often living with us; those cousins, some of whom were older than me, were more like brothers and sisters.

To an outsider, it might seem that growing up with as many as twenty people crammed in a small house would be a challenge, but

I never viewed it that way. A child becomes easily accustomed to life as it is around her. Having many brothers and sisters and cousins with us was a unique, shared experience. With so many people in a small space, it could have been chaotic, but my grandmother, mother, and my mother's sister imposed a discipline on all of us, whether sibling or cousin, which we adhered to. There was a loving, sharing bond between us and when those of us who have lived into our sixties and seventies get together, we comment on how strong the interaction was between us. This does not mean that we were not "real" children, as we did taunt and tease each other, but usually it was within understood boundaries because neither my mother nor my grandmother nor my aunt was afraid to use the rod.

Privacy could be a real issue in a very large household. Bathing was an example. We would bathe once a week. When we were younger, there was absolutely no privacy in the bathing process and boys and girls could be bathed in our No. 3 washtub, a galvanized tin vessel with universal purposes. When puberty arrived, however, my mother and grandmother respected our need for privacy. The No. 3 tub would be filled with water and put in one of the bedrooms. The door would be closed and we as teenagers and preteens could have our weekly bath without embarrassment.

My mother and I were particularly close. I could always talk to her and confide in her, at least until my teenage years when I became deeply involved in civil rights related issues. Then I knew that I could not always tell my mother about my plans because she would have forbidden me to do what I knew I needed to do. Growing up as I did in a fatherless household, I could neither question nor disobey my mother.

My relationship with my grandmother was very different. For reasons that are unclear, but perhaps because I resembled my dad, my grandmother took a strong dislike to me. I recall as a little child my grandmother teaching my older brother, James, to read and write, but when I looked at her longingly, wishing that she would do the same for me, she forcefully refused, leaving me to fend for myself as I have often done in life. This rejection by my grandmother hurt me deeply. I could not understand then or now how she could treat me so badly, but somehow I knew even then that I had to steel myself and find a way to accomplish what I wanted and needed to accomplish, including at that point learning how to read.

Until around the time I became involved in civil rights, my mother always worked outside the home. She worked as a domestic for a period and also as a cook. The best job she ever had was as a short order cook at a textile company known as Mississippi Box & Crate. She was the sole support for me, my siblings, and our extended family.

Because my mother worked long hours and was gone from the house a great deal of time, my brothers and sisters and I essentially raised each other. There was and remains a close bond between us. We viewed each other as protectors, looking out for each other and making sure that we all did chores around the home and completed homework when we were in school. However, when each of us was old enough to work, even as early as ten years old, we all took jobs.

Despite the lack of any real physical comforts, my memories of childhood are mostly pleasant, without bitterness and anger. It was commonplace on a Sunday afternoon or holiday for my family to gather with aunts, uncles, and cousins to eat, play, laugh, and simply enjoy each other's company. Surrounded by family and the aromas of home-cooking, I felt safe and at ease. In that space, we could remove from our minds the concept of Jim Crow segregation and the prevailing injustice of being born black in the United States of America. I hold onto those memories with every fiber of my being because later in my youth my sense of belonging and safety was shattered.

I also have vivid memories from early childhood of the colors and smells that were a part of the Baertown community. Flowers and greenery were everywhere. Everyone it seemed had a garden from which fruits and vegetables could be eaten during the long and hot summer months and canned for use during winter. Notwithstanding the poverty, Baertown was a vibrant community, very much unlike the communities that exist today. Neighbors looked out for neighbors. Adults policed all children—not just their own. We children looked up to and respected the adults. Most everyone was of limited means, and sharing or bartering was common. As an example, my family, in addition to gardening, raised pigs. No one in my family could slaughter the pigs, but we had a neighbor who assumed that awful task. In exchange, we would give him some of the benefits of the slaughter, such as the feet and intestines.

Like many of the other homes in Baertown, ours was heated with a wood stove. There was no running water; we had to draw buckets of water from a neighbor's well and carry them home. We would wash our clothes—the one set of clothes that each of us had—in that same No. 3 washtub in the backyard, where we would heat the water by a wood fire around the tub and wash the clothes using lye. The process was complicated and all of us were involved. Initially, the articles of clothing had to be scrubbed by hand on a washboard. From there, the clothes went into the No. 3 tub. From the No. 3 tub, they went into a cast-iron wash pot filled with lye soap, the only form of soap our family could afford, and we could afford it because our mother made it. From the wash pot, the clothes went through a rinsing process before we would hang them on the outdoor clothesline. Clothes and shoes had to be well taken care of, as they were handed down from family member to family member—we could not afford to have them wear out. Our shoes often had to be bolstered with cardboard inserts to insure that they would last as long as possible.

While we had our garden and our pigs, food was not always readily available for such a large family. At times, my mother or grandmother would bake a hoecake on our wood stove. The hoecake would be cut in pieces, one for each of us, and we were encouraged to eat it quickly and drink a lot of water, as it would fill us up and we could go off to work or school or play as if we had eaten a full meal.

To the residents of Baertown, religion was as important as community. My family attended church every Sunday and we were all expected to be there. As small as our community was, there were six black churches in Baertown. The black churches were: Church of God in Christ; St. Mary I Free Will Baptist; St. Mary II Free Will Baptist; Society Hill Missionary Baptist; Tyree African Methodist Episcopal; and a Holiness Church. My family had a rather eclectic view of religion, unique for its time and even for today. Although we never attended the Church of God in Christ, we would attend any of the other black churches. It did not matter to us which church we attended—all worshipped the same God.

From early on in my church attendance, I recall that from time to time, C. C. Bryant, a deacon at one of the churches, would speak to the congregation and urge the members to register to vote. That is my earliest recollection of anyone speaking out about civil rights.

While racism was prevalent and virulent in McComb and in Mississippi in general, I had no real awareness of it. I grew up in an all-black community, and everyone I knew and interacted with was black. I knew little of the white world or of white people generally. I harbored no anger or bitterness toward whites, despite the fact that my family's situation was deeply affected by the racism in my state, including the fact that my dad could not live with us. We never talked about racism as a concept or a reality. Racism was simply what it was, something that just had to be accepted. My anger and awakening were soon to come.

3

My Education, Brown, *and Emmett Till*

McComb and its environs were not cotton-raising areas, so its elementary and high schools operated differently from those in other areas of Mississippi. Its schools would open in September and remain open through the end of May. But in the cotton growing areas of Mississippi—for example, in the Delta, where my parents migrated before I was born—schools for blacks would not open until cotton picking was finished in October or November. The schools closed again in late March or early April, when cotton planting and cotton chopping, began. White school officials did not stress book learning for blacks; young black people in the Delta obtained education on a "catch as catch can" basis.

My first schooling was in a small house-type building called "the Hut." All of my classmates were black, as were all of my teachers. Later, a new, stark, gray block school was built for black students. It was called Universal Elementary, which was ironic as the only population it served was a black one. My siblings and I walked to elementary school (later we would ride a bus to high school).

The black elementary schools were founded on a strict discipline system. I recall well my first grade teacher, Mrs. Parham. She had a cow bell that she used to organize us. When the bell rang, we would have to line up and march 1-2-3-4 like toy soldiers. We risked harsh discipline if we ever stepped out of line.

My elementary school days were enjoyable. I thrived as a student. I had many good friends in school, some of whom would later join in my civil rights exploits. I recall field trips to the National Cemetery in Vicksburg and the Livingston Park Zoo in Jackson. My basic impression of my early education is that our teachers were trying to prepare us, as best they could, to live as disciplined lives as possible, to never step out of line for fear of what we would incur.

While our elementary school building was a new building, its furnishings were typical of black schools in Mississippi generally. Our desks came from the white schools after they obtained new ones. Some were broken, many were carved up. Similarly, our books were worn, torn, and tattered—discards from the white children after they received new books at their schools.

In May 1954, when I was nine years old, the United States Supreme Court announced its decision in *Brown v. Board of Education*, striking down the separate but equal doctrine*, at least as it related to schooling. Many of my contemporaries in the civil rights movement, like John Lewis, for example, have said that when they first heard about the *Brown* decision, they believed it would make a significant difference in their lives. John, now a distinguished congressman from Georgia, was living in rural Alabama at the time. He wrote in his autobiography that he was stunned and jubilant when he heard of the decision of the Court, believing that soon he would no longer be riding a rickety school bus to "attend classes at a training school with hand-me-down books and supplies" but instead would be "riding a state-of-the-art bus to a state-of-the-art school, an integrated school."

That didn't happen for him—or for his peers for many more years—but nonetheless what was for Congressman Lewis a watershed event in his life was a non-event in my life. I would later

---

* established in 1896 in *Plessy v. Ferguson*.

understand that whites in Mississippi played a significant role in resisting the Court's decision in *Brown*, but in my Baertown community, I had no awareness that the decision had even been announced. I don't know if my mother and grandmother were even aware of it, but what I do know is that they never talked about it with me or my brothers and sisters. None of my teachers or friends in school talked about it either. In Mississippi in 1954, the notion that my friends or I would ever attend schools with white students was not even imaginable, and that was still the case when I reached high school in 1959.

High school was a new awakening for me. I attended Burglund High School along with seven hundred other black students. The school drew its students from all the black neighborhoods of Mc-Comb as well as other areas, including Summit. While all of my friends from Universal Elementary School attended Burglund High, the influx of students from other areas widened my circle of friends

I was a very good student in high school, as was my brother James, two years older than me. I excelled in all my subjects, particularly mathematics, and my mother was always proud of how well I was doing. I became involved in student activities and played on the school basketball team against other African American schools in our area.

Because of my mother's limited income, neither my brother nor I could afford to bring a lunch to school or to buy a school lunch. I volunteered to bus tables and clean up in the school cafeteria. In return, the school gave me a free lunch and also let James eat. It was the only way either of us would have had something to eat to get us through the school day.

WHILE THE *Brown* DECISION didn't make much difference in our lives at the time, a much more immediately impactful event—that would play a pivotal role in my life—occurred a year after *Brown*,

when I was ten. This was the murder of someone not much older
than me—Emmett Till. The story of his murder in Money, Mississippi, in the Delta, has been written about by many authors over
the years. Only recently has his cousin, Simeon Wright, corrected
some of the myths and misconceptions about Emmett's murder.
Simeon was in the Wrights' crowded house and was sleeping in the
same bed with Emmett when the killers came and dragged him
away that night. Simeon had been with Emmett at Milam's Store
that afternoon when the alleged offense took place. Simeon states
that he did not witness any flirtatious conduct by Emmett toward
a white woman, nor did he hear the alleged "wolf whistle" which
was claimed to be the reason Emmett had to die.

But he did die, and the photographs of his mutilated body
that appeared in the September 15, 1955, *Jet* magazine indelibly
imprinted on my psyche and that of many others in my age group.
We could see ourselves and our siblings in those pictures. Another
of my civil rights contemporaries, Carlotta Walls-Lanier, was one
of the Little Rock Nine who integrated Central High School in
1957. She later wrote of seeing the pictures for the first time in *Jet*:

> As horrible as those images were in my imagination, noth-
> ing could have prepared me for the real-life pictures I saw when
> mother's September 15, 1955 issue of *Jet* magazine arrived at our
> home. As I flipped open the magazine and turned to the story
> about Emmett Till's memorial service, I gasped. The photo of his
> badly disfigured corpse was right there, in black and white. Part
> of me was so horrified that I wanted to turn the page quickly
> or throw the book down, but I couldn't take my eyes off his
> bloated, monstrous face. It was one of those moments when
> legend meets reality.

Her reaction exactly mirrored my own. I could not believe that anyone could be so cruel or so evil as to turn the smiling face of someone my age into something wholly unrecognizable as human.

Unlike the *Brown* decision, the murder of Emmett Till was talked about at length within my family. My mother and grandmother kept reiterating that whatever he did, he was still "just a boy, just a boy." In reading the article which accompanied the photos, I saw the term "wolf whistle" and had no idea what it meant or why someone should be killed for it. I remember asking my grandmother what wolf whistle meant. No satisfactory explanation could be offered.

Many of my friends were traumatized by the photos of Emmett. Some parents even used the photos as a life-learning lesson for young black boys, or black men, for that matter—step out of line and you might be the next person whose death photo would appear in *Jet*. Others, like Carlotta Walls-Lanier's family, chose to not even travel through Mississippi. But while Mississippi evoked fear in the hearts of some, I lived there. The death and the photos had an opposite effect on me. Perhaps Emmett's mother knew that by showing her son's desecrated body, some people would merely recoil in fear and horror but for others it would have the opposite effect—outrage and anger. That was my reaction.

I had never been an angry person. But the raw brutality of Emmett Till's murder unleashed something in me. I recognized and felt the third- or fourth-class citizenship that my family and I had to endure. How easy was it for two white men to grab a young black man from his bed and murder him because he had, in their opinion, somehow stepped out of line? My own father had to flee—with me inside my mother—for having somehow stepped out of line. I was only ten when Emmett Till was killed, but somehow I resolved at that tender age that I was going to channel the anger boiling up inside of me, and I was going to do something to make my life, my mother's life, my father's life somehow better. I had no idea how I was going to accomplish it, but I knew that I would find a way to do something meaningful with my life to better the world of Mississippi that we had to endure.

But before I would find my way, the Emmett Till story became even more real for me and my family. It was 6 a.m. on a morning a couple of months after the Till murder, which was still on everyone's mind. My mother was at work on her night shift as a cook. The rest of the family was at home asleep. My brother, James, not quite thirteen years old at the time, was sleeping on a pull-out couch in the living room. I was asleep on another couch in the living room. All of a sudden a number of white McComb police officers broke open the door of our house and came running in. Several other officers remained outside. My grandmother was up and got in the way of the officers and asked what they were doing breaking into her house. They pushed her aside, saying "Shut up, old lady." They went to the couch where James, was sleeping and, as had happened to Emmett Till, they snatched him out of his bed. Without saying a word to the rest of us, they led him out of the house and into the night. I watched, as Simeon Wright before me had watched, as my brother was taken away. We all witnessed what happened, but in an instant James was gone, and we were left with our thoughts and fears. Needless to say, my family was traumatized. We believed that we would never see James again, as Emmett Till and countless other black men and women had never been seen again after they were seized for some alleged indiscretion.

The timing of this incident could not have been worse. I could not get the image of the brutally beaten Emmett Till out of my head. I kept imagining my brother, whom I adored, being brutalized and killed. My grandmother was distraught as was my mother when she came home. We all believed that we had seen my brother alive for the last time.

Some hours later, much to our joy and relief, James came walking in the door. We all hugged him and cried for the grandson,

son, and brother whom we had given up for dead. My brother did not want to talk about what had occurred, and at the time we were just so happy to have him home that no one pressed him to talk. It was only many years later that my brother would reluctantly open up about the incident, because he had been filled with the same dread that had flooded us—that he would meet the same fate as Emmett Till. He has since told me that the police accused him of stealing. While he never acknowledged that he was physically assaulted by the police, he did say that the police did everything that they could to terrorize him and frighten him into a confession. Much to my brother's credit at his young age, he refused to give in to the pressure and said that he just could not confess to doing something he did not do. The police ultimately gave up and let him go, not even having the decency to bring him back home, but making him walk on his own.

The Emmett Till murder, combined with our own family's terrifying experience, steeled my resolve to do something—anything—to change the brutal world blacks were forced to endure. At age ten, maybe I was older and wiser than my years, but I somehow knew that my opportunity would come to make a difference. The way was not clear, but the resolve was clear.

The way presented itself some years later when the civil rights movement came to McComb.

4

The Civil Rights Movement Comes to McComb

In addition to my work in the high school cafeteria, I also worked outside of school. Whatever child labor laws may have existed in the 1950s and early '60s were mostly ignored in Mississippi. So I was allowed to work as a short-order cook and at other jobs to bolster my mother's meager income. At the same time, I was eager for outside activities and experiences. I knew that Mr. C. C. Bryant headed the Pike County NAACP branch, and I had heard him exhorting church members to join the NAACP and register to vote. I thus looked to Mr. Bryant to help direct the nascent force inside of me that wanted to change how my people were treated in Baertown and the larger McComb community.

Mr. Bryant suggested that an NAACP youth committee be formed and he named me its president. The only other member of that committee at the time was Mr. Bryant's son, Curtis. When he set up the NAACP youth committee and appointed me its president, Mr. Bryant did not tell me what was expected of me, but somehow I knew that this new role would lead in some wonderful way to my finding a path to make a difference. That was to come very soon. Although later on I didn't tell my mother about my civil rights activities, I did tell her about becoming the head of the Pike County NAACP youth committee. She was proud and supportive.

While there were faint rumblings in some areas of Mississippi to bring about change, the real origins of the civil rights movement in the state were right in my hometown of McComb. Much has been written about the iconic role of Bob Moses in the civil rights movement, and those of us who have known him and loved him for many years feel that the accolades bestowed upon him are well-deserved, for he was a pioneer in bringing an awakening to a people in the most godforsaken state in the U.S.—Mississippi.

While much is known about Bob, few realize that his start as a civil rights revolutionary came about in McComb. And while many of the books about the movement point to the iconic figure of Robert Moses as the person who spearheaded McComb's civil rights efforts, Bob, in his typical insightful view of things, takes no such credit. Instead, he points to C. C. Bryant as being most responsible for the movement's initial forays into hostile, violence-prone McComb. Bob has been quoted as saying:

> Last night there was a statement made that I initiated or started the movement, but anyone who thinks must know that I couldn't have done that because I wasn't from McComb. And as far as I know things don't get started by somebody who is not from someplace, just going in cold turkey and figuring that they are going to start something. And C. C. Bryant was the person who actually started this thing.

Without the incredible bravery of both C. C. Bryant and Bob Moses, my life would not be what it is today. A confluence of events—my budding desire to become involved in something greater than myself, and Bob's arrival in McComb—created the vehicle I was seeking to bring about change in the McComb community.

BOB'S FIRST EXPOSURE TO civil rights came in early 1960, as it did for many others in the movement. In February 1960 four black students at North Carolina Agricultural and Technical College (A&T) sought service at a whites-only lunch counter in a Woolworth's department store in Greensboro, North Carolina. This spontaneous and courageous act by the four young men sparked a sit-in movement throughout the South, including in Nashville, Tennessee, where a group of young people had been preparing for months to begin similar protests.

While these events were going on throughout the South and were being broadcast throughout the nation, a young teacher in New York City saw the photographs of the student demonstrations. They ignited something within Bob Moses, who would later say: "I could feel myself in the faces of the people that they had there on the front pages. I could feel how they felt, just by looking at the pictures." In the same way the police taking away my brother had inspired me to action, the photographs of the sit-ins inspired Bob to become involved in the burgeoning civil rights movement.

Bob's initial steps were tentative. On spring break in 1960, he went to Virginia where he participated for the first time in a picket line. While on the picket line, he met a representative of the Southern Christian Leadership Conference (SCLC), the organization headed by Martin Luther King Jr., fresh off his historic leadership of the Montgomery Bus Boycott in Alabama. When the school year ended in 1960, Bob traveled to Atlanta to SCLC headquarters to work for the summer in its civil rights activities in the South.

That summer, SCLC and the recently formed Student Nonviolent Coordinating Committee (SNCC) were working more closely together than they would in later years. SNCC planned to hold a conference in the fall of 1960 and wanted to invite black leaders throughout the South to become a part of this "local people"-driven organization. Bob Moses was sent to Mississippi to recruit attendees for the conference. This was Bob's introduction to my home state, the most intransigent in the nation, and it would lead him to spend the next four to five years trying to bring change to it.

In his initial Mississippi foray, Bob met with Amzie Moore, C. C. Bryant's counterpart in the Delta. Like Bryant, Moore had been active in the NAACP for years. While for the most part those were years of frustration, Moore saw in the student sit-ins the way to bring about change.

However, Moore's vision differed from that of the student activists. He saw no benefit for most black folk in being able to buy a hamburger at a lunch counter, because most black Mississippians—including my family—could not afford to buy a Coke, let alone a burger. Much like Bryant, Moore envisioned change as being accomplished through obtaining power, and the only way black folk could obtain power was through the vote. Moore believed that by enlisting young people such as Bob Moses and student leaders in voter registration activities, true change would be effected. He invited Bob to come back in 1961 to register black voters. Bob agreed. He returned to New York at the end of the summer to complete his two-year commitment as a teacher in the New York public schools but vowed to return to Mississippi in 1961.

An article in *Jet*, the same magazine in which I had seen the horrific pictures of Emmett Till, told about Bob's proposed venture in Mississippi. The article indicated that he would be working through SNCC to start a drive to register voters in Mississippi Delta towns in the summer of 1961. C. C. Bryant saw the *Jet* article. As Bob had been inspired by articles about the sit-ins, Mr. Bryant was inspired by this article and reached out to Amzie Moore in the Delta. Mr. Bryant wanted to bring someone to McComb to work on what he had been preaching about for years—the necessity of getting black people registered to vote.

Mr. Bryant's contact with Mr. Moore was fortuitous. When Bob arrived in Mr. Moore's hometown, Cleveland, Mississippi, in

1961, Mr. Moore said he did not believe that his community was ready for a voter registration drive. While Mr. Moore had worked in his steadfast way through the fall, winter, and spring of 1960–61 to inspire his community to embrace a commitment to registering voters, he had concluded after many months that his community was simply not ready.

When Bob arrived in Cleveland that summer to begin what he expected to be a voter registration movement in the Delta, he soon learned from Mr. Moore that it was not to be. However, Mr. Moore recommended that Bob travel to McComb and meet with Mr. Bryant, who had assured Mr. Moore that McComb *was* ready to begin a civil rights revolution focusing on voter registration.

Thus, the civil rights movement first came to McComb.

WHILE I CANNOT BE certain, I believe that the first day that Bob arrived in McComb was the first day I met him. It was a magical day that started out badly but had a dramatic turn that would ultimately change the course of my life. I was sixteen years old in the summer of 1961. I had been working two jobs to help out my family. I continued to work as a short-order cook and also worked at a dry cleaners as a presser. On the fateful day of my first meeting Bob, I was working at the cleaners. My boss was a white woman. I never knew her last name, but her first name was Sadie, and that's what we called her behind her back. To her face, of course, we called her "Miss Sadie," in accord with the Jim Crow customs of the time.

While I was pressing one of the garments some wrinkles resulted, which are referred to as a "cat face." When Sadie saw the "cat face" in the garment, she threatened me. She told me that if I did not get the wrinkle out of the garment, she was going to kick my behind so hard my nose would bleed. I was more angry than intimidated by the remark, and I dropped what I was doing and walked out, never to return. Because I was still waiting to hear from Mr. Bryant about what role he planned for me as NAACP youth council president, I walked from the cleaners to Mr. Bryant's home. Fate was on my side.

When I arrived at Mr. Bryant's, he invited me in and introduced me to Bob Moses. He told me that Bob was from New York but had come to McComb to help set up a voter registration project. I was mesmerized as I listened to Mr. Bryant and Mr. Moses talk about their plans. I listened intently as Bob talked about setting up schools to educate people on the voter registration process. That process was incredibly intimidating for any black residents, as it involved knowing the Mississippi Constitution and being able to interpret any given section at the whim of the (white) registrar.

I was in awe of the quiet, soft-spoken man. It was as if my prayers had been answered. This young man, a stranger to our community, was outlining a plan that promised to make life better for me and for all of the people in Baertown and McComb. While he may have been a stranger, he was like a native son to me. I was thrilled when he and Mr. Bryant invited me to become involved in the voter registration campaign, as Mr. Bryant told Bob that I was well known in the McComb community and that I could help him acquaint Bob with the McComb community and introduce him to people who would likely become involved in the voter registration drive. I knew then what my role would be as the president of the NAACP youth committee.

With C. C. Bryant's assistance and that of other prominent members of the McComb black community, including Mr. Webb Owens, a center of operations was established for this new voter registration drive. As Mr. Owens was a Mason, he persuaded the black Masons to open the doors of their Masonic Temple for Bob and other activists to work from.

The Masonic Temple became my home away from home. I spent every waking hour that summer at the Masonic Temple or out canvassing the community. Besides Bob Moses, other important SNCC activists arrived in McComb including Chuck McDew, Charles Jones, Travis Britt, Cordell Reagon, and Bernard and Colia Lafayette. While most were somewhat older than I was, they were not appreciably so, and all of them made me feel that I was an integral part of the mission.

In our initial work at the Masonic Temple, the SNCC workers trained me and others on the process of canvassing to invite people to attend meetings at the Masonic Temple. At the meetings, the SNCC workers and recruits would talk to the people about the importance of registering to vote, how the vote could liberate them, and the steps necessary to go about registering, including the oppressively burdensome constitutional interpretation requirement. To encourage participation, fliers were drafted which told about the almost nightly meetings at the Masonic Temple for voter registration classes. I recruited friends to help in the canvassing process and met others like me—including Hollis Watkins and Curtis Hayes—who had heard about the voter registration drive and eagerly joined it.

The SNCC workers also trained us on how to stress to our people why they should come to the meetings at the Masonic Temple. They would send us out usually in pairs to canvass throughout the three black neighborhoods in McComb, although I was so enthralled about the work that if there was no one to go out with me, I would go alone. The process was tedious but so uplifting that I did not often notice Mississippi's extreme temperatures of July and August because I had found what I believed that God had ordained me to do.

I always kept an upbeat composure, even if I got discouraged at times when people saw me and the others coming, knew who we were and knew why we were coming, but would turn away, or retreat into their homes, or just plain tell us that they didn't want to fool with this registration business. We knew these reactions were because fear reigned supreme.

WE HAD SOME INITIAL success in our voter registration efforts. After the first training classes, four people went to the county seat, which is in Magnolia, to attempt to register to vote. Three passed the voter registration test. Two days later, three more people went to Magnolia and two of the three passed.

But on the third day, a Thursday, nine people went down to register. By this time the local white authorities were becoming aware that something must be going on. Why else would sixteen black residents have come in to register to vote when over the years virtually none had done so. On this Thursday, the authorities only registered one of the nine, and information was provided to the local newspaper, the *McComb Enterprise-Journal*. The *Journal* published an article about the number of blacks who were showing up to register to vote, in effect warning the white community about what was transpiring in the black community. That led, of course, to reprisals against those of us who were involved, the SNCC workers, and more importantly the initial brave people who had overcome the rampant fear in the black community and had gone to Magnolia to attempt to register.

While I am sure that the *Enterprise-Journal* viewed its article as a call to arms in the white community, it had the opposite effect in the black community in McComb and particularly in the two counties that border Pike, Amite and Walthall counties. While McComb in 1961 seemed almost progressive with 250 black registered voters, in Amite and Walthall counties there were none. If McComb was violence prone, Amite and Walthall were even worse. Some incredibly brave people in Amite County, including E. W. Steptoe, who had been active in the NAACP, reached out to C. C. Bryant to bring Bob Moses to help them get people in that county registered.

Bob was fully aware of the even greater danger posed by going into Amite County. Pike County had McComb, a fairly large urban community by Mississippi standards. But Amite and Walthall counties were very rural, with many organized Klan-related groups whose memberships included many of the prominent local citizens and politicians. However, Bob knew that despite the danger, he and the civil rights movement could not reject a call for help. So Bob himself went to Amite County, and with Mr. Steptoe and Mr. Louis Allen's help, he began working with and educating interested county residents on the voter registration process.

In mid-August, Bob, along with three Amite County volunteers, went to the courthouse in the county seat, a town ironically named Liberty. This was the town where my mother was born. When they arrived at the courthouse and went to the registrar's office, the registrar, in a hostile tone, asked the volunteers why they were there. The volunteers were struck with fear, but Bob, who was never intimidated by even the most hateful of white officials, responded calmly that the people had come to register to vote. The registrar stared at Bob and questioned why he was with the local people, and then he told them they would have to wait.

The wait lasted hours, with various county and other officials, including a Mississippi highway patrolman, periodically walking through the registrar's offices, glaring hatefully at Bob and the volunteers. After many hours, the first volunteers from Amite County were allowed to fill out the registration form. For any black person from Amite County, that in itself was an incredible accomplishment, even though they knew they would likely never be approved to vote.

Feeling some elation, Bob and the volunteers left the courthouse. In short order they were brought down from their high spirits, as a highway patrolman followed them from the courthouse and stayed on their tail for many miles, finally pulling the car over and arresting Bob for the baseless charge of "interfering with an officer in the performance of his duties."

Shortly after his arrest, Bob was brought to trial, convicted, and fined $50. When he refused to pay the fine, it was reduced to $5, and when Bob still refused to pay it, he was sent to jail. After two days in jail, Bob's fine was paid by an NAACP attorney from Jackson, and Bob was released.

This may have been the first arrest of Bob Moses for civil rights-related activities, but it would by no means be his last. Bob was undaunted and knew that he had to return to Amite County as soon as possible to insure that the black folks of the county knew that he was not afraid and neither should they be. Mr. Steptoe arranged for Bob to set up voter registration classes in a Baptist church in a remote location where the authorities would be unlikely to learn of the activities. After two weeks of regular meetings, two additional people, Curtis Dawson and a man known as Preacher Knox, agreed to try to register to vote.

On the day set for Bob and the two men to go to the courthouse in Liberty, upon their arrival at the courthouse, they found the sidewalk blocked by three white men who somehow had found out that the group was coming. The three white men, a son and two cousins of the Amite County sheriff, asked Moses where they were going. When Bob replied that they were going to the registrar's office, one of the men, Billy Jack Caston, told him, "No," and struck Bob in the forehead with the blunt end of a knife. Almost knocked unconscious by the blow, Bob fell. Caston continued to beat him about the head. As Bob lay on the ground, bleeding profusely, he could hear Mr. Dawson pleading with Caston to stop. He could also hear the footsteps of his attackers as they ran off.

With the help of Mr. Dawson, Bob was able to get to his feet. Despite the blood pouring down his face and onto his clothes, he told Mr. Dawson that they could not be deterred but must proceed to the registrar's office. Bob was heartened that both Mr. Dawson and Mr. Knox agreed to continue.

When they went into the office, even the cold-hearted registrar could not help but be stunned by this bloody, soft-spoken man, whom he had seen some time before, indicating that Mr. Dawson and Mr. Knox were there to register to vote. Taken aback, the registrar told the men to leave and closed the office.

Later, Bob filed a complaint against Caston for beating him. This was an even more incredibly brave thing to do, as black men in Mississippi in that time dared not seek redress when attacked by white men. As could be expected, a perfunctory trial of Caston was held and an all-white jury found him not guilty. But Bob Moses had set a precedent. He served as an example to the people of Amite County that despite whites' violent, oppressive tactics, a black man with courage could stand up to them. It was truly inspiring for all of us.

THE EXPERIENCE IN WALTHALL County was not much different from what occurred in Amite County. While Bob Moses focused his attention on Amite County, John Hardy, MacArthur Cotton, Jimmie Travis, and George Lowe* ventured into Walthall County to set up a registration school. The irrepressible C. C. Bryant made a contact for them in Walthall with his uncle, Robert Bryant. After a series of training classes, two potential applicants, Edith Peters and Lucius Wilson, who were fairly economically independent because they owned their own farms, agreed to accompany Hardy to the courthouse in the county seat of Tylertown.

When the trio entered the registrar's office, Registrar John Q. Wood refused to give applications to Peters and Wilson. When

---

* Hardy was a veteran of the Nashville sit-ins; Cotton, Travis, and Lowe were students from Jackson, the state capital.

Hardy attempted to intervene, the registrar pulled a pistol and pointed it at Hardy and the applicants, then ordered them out of his offices. As the three were walking out the door of the offices, the registrar came up behind Hardy and gave him a mighty blow on the back of his head with the gun. With the assistance of Peters and Wilson, the bleeding Hardy staggered out the door.

Peters and Wilson wanted to take Hardy to a doctor, but Hardy, recalling what Moses had done when attacked by Caston, insisted that he wanted to go to the sheriff's office and swear out a complaint against the registrar. However, before he could get to the sheriff's office, Sheriff Edd Craft came looking for him. Rather than processing a complaint against the registrar, the sheriff arrested Hardy on a charge of disturbing the peace and jailed him.

That night, the sheriff, having heard rumors that a lynch mob was forming to take Hardy from the jail, moved him in the still of the night to the Pike County jail in Magnolia. This was an inexplicable move by a white Mississippi sheriff of that time, but otherwise John Hardy probably would have become another of the many martyrs of the civil rights movement.

Ultimately the charges against Hardy were dropped due to intervention by the U.S. Justice Department. This was a rare instance of the federal government taking any action to protect a civil rights worker in Mississippi in this era. The Justice Department asserted that the federally protected right to vote of the black people of Walthall County was at issue if John was required to stand trial and that the county's black population's federal right to register to vote would be inhibited if the state prosecution went forward.

The point was not about John's rights, but the suit was brought on behalf of the black people of Walthall, and it was an unprecedented action in which the Department of Justice stopped a local criminal prosecution before it went to trial. Issues of federalism versus the constitutional status of the people were at stake.

5

The Emergence of Direct Action

When Bob Moses arrived in 1961, his mission was voter registration, and in his meetings with Amzie Moore and C. C. Bryant, there was no discussion about trying to replicate the sit-ins that had engulfed most of the southern states except Mississippi.

Indeed, prior to the late summer of 1961, Mississippi had seen little of what can be described as "direct action," i.e., black people trying to exercise their right to use segregated facilities. The first action was in March 1961, when nine black students from local Tougaloo College entered the segregated public library in Jackson, the state capital. Before the authorities realized what was taking place, the students took books off the library shelves and sat peacefully to read. As would be the pattern in other actions in Mississippi, the nine were arrested. Besides the Jackson library sit-in, the other notable direct action in the state involved the Freedom Riders who "invaded" in May through August 1961.* When the Freedom Riders exited their buses in Jackson, they were immediately arrested and taken to prison. Mississippi remained the "closed society," as it was labeled by the historian James Silver.

While Bob's focus was on voter registration, his concept of how

---

* A continuation of the planned Washington, D.C., to New Orleans bus ride by activists sponsored by CORE and the Fellowship of Reconciliation.

Mississippi could be attacked was not shared by all in SNCC. During the summer of 1961, SNCC's expanding membership met at the Highlander Folk School in Tennessee. At that meeting, the young activists formed into two camps. One group was led by those who agreed with Bob that voter registration was the appropriate vehicle to break open Mississippi's closed society. The other group, many of whom had been involved in the Nashville Movement, wanted to bring to Mississippi and other Deep South states their model of direct action against segregated public and private facilities.

The tension between these competing factions almost tore SNCC apart, but Ella Baker, "the mother of the civil rights movement," wisely intervened, as she was to do in so many situations. She suggested that two wings be created within SNCC. One would focus on voter registration in the Bob Moses mold. The other wing would create a plan to "Move on Mississippi," which would be a massive desegregation effort against all the institutions in the state. Most members of this latter group, including Nashville Movement stalwarts Diane Nash and James Bevel, centered their activities in Jackson.

However, another of SNCC's Nashville veterans, Marion Barry, came to McComb to recruit its young people into the "Move on Mississippi" program. Barry was somewhat reluctantly received by Bob Moses, but he was enthusiastically received by many of us younger people of McComb.

Bob was concerned that sit-ins and protests in McComb would not necessarily result in any real change. But ultimately he acquiesced in such activity because he recognized that many of us who had been working tirelessly, albeit frustratingly, in the voter registration campaign viewed the concept of sit-ins as a direct attack on the system that perpetuated our second-class citizenship.

BARRY AND OTHER SNCC activists set up training programs for

us at the Masonic Temple. The "direct action" training programs differed greatly from what we had been taught in our voter registration classes. Much of the direct action training involved role playing. Those of us who expressed an interest—and there were far fewer than had expressed interest in voter registration—were put in situations that resembled what would occur if we tried to use the white facilities in a restaurant or a bus station. We were trained to be nonviolent but to expect violence.

We were taught how to enter a facility with our heads up but to be mindful that not only would there be hateful stares from the whites who were in the facilities, probably there would also be catcalls and jeering and attacks on our personhood. We were instructed not to react in a self-defensive manner but to accept as a given a violent attack for the audacity of us trying to break down what belonged only to whites. SNCC instructors would take the roles of white onlookers and bystanders, screaming racist statements at us and attacking us. We learned how to assume a fetal position—to roll up into a ball to protect somewhat our heads and organs from a likely beating.

We were also trained to expect to go to jail. J-A-I-L was a four-letter word that invoked fear in the hearts and minds of black folk. John Lewis, the heroic leader of SNCC, relates the challenge that the idea of going to jail presented to him and other young black men who became involved in the movement. While the reality was and is that young black men too often wind up in jail—and too often for unjustified causes—being jailed still carries a stigma in the black community.

For those like John and me, who came from families that were proud that none of their members had gone to jail, willingly going to jail was a difficult but necessary concept to overcome. Yet we knew that any direct action, any attempt to desegregate a facility, could well result in our being jailed. In one way, it was a nightmare, but in another way it was an integral part of breaking down the system of segregation.

AFTER MANY TRAINING SESSIONS, the SNCC activists and the McComb young people felt that it was time to put "action" into the concept of direct action. Hollis Watkins and Curtis Hayes, who had worked with me in the voter registration project, volunteered to go into the Woolworth's store in downtown McComb and, like their predecessors in Greensboro, North Carolina, seek service at the whites-only lunch counter. However, Hollis and Curtis were treated very differently from how the Greensboro students had been. In Greensboro the students sat-in and were not served, but left at the end of the day only to return the next day. Mississippi is not North Carolina. When Hollis and Curtis sat-in at the McComb Woolworth's lunch counter, the first ever restaurant sit-in in Mississippi, the police were immediately called and Hollis and Curtis were arrested for disturbing the peace and taken to jail in the county seat in Magnolia.

A day or two after Hollis and Curtis were arrested, a large meeting was held at the Masonic Temple with over two hundred locals, including me, in attendance. James Bevel, a fiery SNCC orator who was then working in Jackson, came down to McComb and exhorted the crowd not to let Hollis and Curtis sit alone in jail, but to follow up and take additional direct action. Bob Moses, who had just returned that day from his beating in Liberty, also urged the people not to give up and stressed the importance of continuing to take action to show black people that a little adversity, such as a jailing and a beating, was not going to stop the movement. As the meeting continued that night, the concept of a follow-up to the Woolworth's sit-in was developed. The new target was the Greyhound bus station. Volunteers were sought to go into the Greyhound bus station and seek to buy tickets at the white counter to travel to Tennessee. Although the crowd exceeded two hundred, only three people volunteered: Bobby Talbert; Ike Lewis, a fellow student at Burglund High School; and me. I was the only girl to volunteer and the only minor.

It is interesting that some of the most important decisions that we make in life, that impact our lives forever, are made quickly and instinctively. I had no idea when I volunteered along with Ike and Bobby that this decision would set the course for my life. I knew that my decision was right, knew intellectually and emotionally that it was necessary for someone to step forward at great risk and that someone was me. While I did not, could not, fully appreciate the risk that I was taking as a sixteen-year-old girl, I knew that everything I had experienced in life up to this time was moving me in this direction. And I was comfortable in myself that what I was doing was not only the right thing to do, it was the only thing to do.

In light of the uproar that took place after Bobby, Ike, and I attempted to integrate the bus station the next day, it is important to set the record straight on two issues that over the years have been incorrectly written about my involvement. First of all, I was sixteen, not fifteen, as many books have stated. Second, it has been said that I lied about my age, because I knew that if my true age was known, I would not have been allowed to go. This is simply untrue and is likely revisionist history and a reaction to the criticism that the movement received after the fact in McComb, and later in Birmingham and other places, which allowed children to be involved in the movement and to go to jail for it.

I have never lied about my age and certainly would not have lied about it in the context of such an important movement event.

After Bobby, Ike, and I volunteered, we talked at length with the SNCC workers about what we were to do and how we were to go to the bus station and attempt to buy tickets at the white counter.

SNCC gave each of us money to buy a ticket. When I went home that night, I had a feeling of exhilaration in anticipation of what was going to take place the next day. While I had never been to the bus station before, and I had never been to jail before, the two were inextricably bound together, as I knew that at the end of the day that followed my ultimate destination was jail.

Thinking about Hollis and Curtis and Bob, who had also been jailed, I was not fearful; I knew what I was doing was what God wanted me to do. It was the right thing and I was doing the right thing. I knew that many people who became involved in the movement lost jobs or had family members who lost jobs.

As I packed the only thing I planned to take with me to the bus station—an extra pair of underwear—I thought of how my mother worked and sacrificed for all of us. But I knew what I was doing had to be done, whatever the consequences might be.

I kissed my mother that night and hugged her tightly, saying nothing about what was going to happen the next day. I knew that I would probably not see her again for quite a while.

As I went to bed, I prayed to God for my family and for me, to protect us and keep us safe.

6

My First Arrest and Jail Time

The next day, Bobby, Ike and I met at the Masonic Temple. After receiving words of encouragement from the SNCC workers, we walked to the bus station. Bobby, as the oldest, led the way. When we entered the station, no one paid any attention to the three "colored" youths. The whites present would soon be calling us the N-word (or, as I prefer to think of it, the No-word), but they ignored us until we walked over to the whites-only counter. Then we became the focus of everyone's attention in the station.

Hateful glances and stares attempted to pierce right though us. A growing murmur of disgust rose, and the "No-word" began to be shouted with vigor. Before we could even answer why we were there, the police arrived and arrested us. While the police did not appreciate their role that day, in a sense they were our rescuers, because I am convinced that the whites present at the station were ready and prepared to act out their murmurs and shouts.

We were taken to the McComb city jail and booked and put in holding cells. Then we were taken from McComb to the county jail in Magnolia. Bobby, Ike, and I talked while at the McComb police station and on the way to Magnolia, with Bobby in his inimitable manner cracking jokes and making light of the first time any of us had ever been to jail. There was a peace in our hearts as we knew that we had taken a dramatic step to make our world and the world for blacks and whites a better place to be.

It is hard to explain how I, as a sixteen-year-old, felt as I was led into the Pike County Jail. While everything in my upbringing told me that jail was a place where neither I nor my brothers or sisters should ever wind up, here I was, in jail, occupying a segregated cell with another black woman, and I was totally at peace. The SNCC workers had trained me well. They had talked about how their experiences in the movement inevitably led them to be jailed. While being arrested was not a badge of honor, and jail could be a very dangerous place—as evidenced by many of them being beaten while in jail—it was a necessary part of the process to bring about change.

I felt good about what I had done and felt that I was standing in the shoes of many black people who came before me. Martin Luther King described his first jailing in a way that I can fully understand: "Ordinarily leaving a court room with a conviction behind him a man would wear a somber face. But I left with a smile. I knew that I was convicted criminal, but I was proud of my crime." While I had never been convicted of a crime, I knew I was in jail for taking an important step in the liberation of my people and all people.

I soon became aware of how dangerous a prison can be. As the only woman involved in the direct action at the Greyhound station, I was housed on the first floor while Bobby and Ike were in cells for males on the second floor. Like the rest of Mississippi, the cells were segregated. My cellmate was another black female. The cell contained two bunk-type cots, one up and one down, a water basin, and a commode. Most of the day, we were locked in our cell together. Shortly after I arrived at the jail, my cellmate told me that the authorities had asked her to physically harm me. In exchange for her beating me, the officials would let her out early for the sentence she was serving. However, she refused to do the bidding of the jail officials. She told me that she knew my family and knew that we were good people. But she also told me that she knew my uncle and feared that if he found out that I had been

Because I was on the first floor and Bobby, Ike, Hollis, and Curtis were on the second floor, being locked up was lonely, particularly after my cellmate was released. I took to sleeping during the day and being awake most of the night. Jail is not a quiet place. The men upstairs would often call down to me to see how I was doing. At night when the lights were turned down, Hollis, Curtis, and the others would start singing freedom songs or songs that we had learned at church that we converted into freedom songs. I would join them in singing "Oh, Freedom" and "This Little Light of Mine," even though there was no light shining in the jail.

Often the guards would try to quiet us, but without any success, as singing was our way of keeping up our spirits and reminding us why we were doing what we were. Because the Pike County Jail was located in an all-white area of Magnolia, apparently many people in the neighborhood complained about our serenading them at night. We enjoyed the irony of being in jail for exercising our rights and even creating additional disturbance while there.

Sometimes I had the good fortune of being able to get out of my cell to go to the men's section to visit with my friends. This was made possible because a family friend, Richard Banks, was one of the trusties. His mother, Rita Banks, was a good friend of my mother, so Richard took me under his wing and gave me privileges that ordinarily I would not have had, including being able to visit Hollis, Bobby, and the others.

I do not know how or when my mother first found out that I was in jail, but it may have been through Mrs. Banks or Bobby Talbert's mother, because Bobby's mom and my mom were like sisters. My mother came to visit me as often as she could, despite the difficulty in getting from McComb to Magnolia—even though the distance was not that great, we had no car nor other means of transportation, and my mother had to rely on friends or other family members to get her there. Our conversations were always warm and loving. My mother never asked me why I had done what I did, but I could tell by her silent, approving manner that she was proud of the stance that I had taken. Sometimes silent communication is the best communication.

I did grieve for my mother as she told me of the threats she was receiving on her jobs and the fear that she had that she would lose her jobs, all because of my actions, and that she would have a difficult time caring for the rest of the family. She wanted me to know, but she also assured me that God would provide for her and the family despite the hardship and made me know implicitly that what I had done was a heroic thing and that the family would survive. She also told me that rumors were being spread throughout the community that her daughter was a "bad" person, not so much because I was in prison, but because I was sexually promiscuous. These lies were not surprising. They were fomented by the Mississippi State Sovereignty Commission, the secret police unit created in 1956 to react aggressively against any perceived challenges to white supremacy. As I have learned since, the Sovereignty Commission was vicious in its actions against any "colored" person or sympathetic white who dared speak out or act out. While I hurt for my mother at the time, I knew then as I know now that for those of us who chose to act on our convictions, the price could be great, not just for us but for our families.

In one of my visits with my mother I was reminded that the price some of us would pay for trying to break down the walls of segregation was the ultimate price—death. We all came to realize that it could happen at any time to any of us. My mother told me that Herbert Lee, one of the independent farmers in Amite County, who along with E. W. Steptoe had introduced Bob Moses to the local black community, had been murdered. Mr. Lee was a young man with nine children. Despite great risk, he had driven Bob

Moses around Amite County when Bob first came there. Word of Mr. Lee's actions had spread to influential people in the white community, one of whom was State Representative E. H. Hurst. Ironically, Hurst and Lee had grown up together and were childhood friends, but by 1961 Hurst was a leading white supremacist who was known for threatening black activists.

On September 25, 1961, Mr. Lee drove a truck-load of cotton to the gin in Liberty, where he encountered Representative Hurst. Witnesses testified at a coroner's hearing that Lee had confronted Hurst and tried to attack him with a tire iron, then Hurst drew his revolver and tried to hit Lee on the head with it, but the gun discharged, killing Lee. But what later emerged was that the death of Herbert Lee was a cold-blooded murder.

Louis Allen, a poor black farmer with a wife and three young children, was at the cotton gin that day and witnessed the murder. He was threatened and coerced into telling the coroner's jury a story that supported Hurst's claim of self-defense. Many black men before and after him had been threatened and coerced in similar circumstances. But when interviewed later by Bob Moses, Allen recounted a very different version of what occurred. He told Bob that Lee did not have a tire iron or any weapon on the day of his murder. Rather, Lee was confronted by Hurst, who was brandishing his pistol. Mr. Lee, with great courage, told Hurst that he was not going to talk to him as long as he had his gun out. Hurst screamed at Lee: "I am not playing with you this morning!" Hurst then shot Lee in the head. Because Mr. Allen was standing nearby when all of this happened, Hurst coached him as to exactly what he should say to the authorities. Out of fear for his own life, Mr. Allen did as he was told.

But later he told Bob Moses the truth, and he was courageous enough to tell the truth to Justice Department representatives and the FBI. When word of this got out, Mr. Allen became a marked man. Like my father, he knew that he had to leave Mississippi. But on the night before he was to leave to begin a new life in Milwaukee, Mr. Allen was shot and killed in the driveway of his home. He thus joined Mr. Lee as one of the many Mississippi martyrs for civil rights, following in the footsteps of the Reverend George Lee, and in turn followed by the murders of Medgar Evers, James Chaney, Michael Schwerner, Andrew Goodman, and Ben Chester White, to name just a few.

AFTER SERVING TWENTY-EIGHT DAYS in jail and having missed the entire first month of school, I was released from jail along with Hollis, Curtis, Bobby, and Ike. Apparently a coalition had been formed involving the NAACP and the Southern Christian Leadership Conference to bail the five of us out of jail. The check written for my bail was signed by Martin Luther King Jr.

I had no idea at the time how short-lived my freedom would be.

7

The Burglund High School Walkout

M y welcome home was extraordinary. There were hugs and kisses from my mother and sisters and brothers. It was good to be out of jail and good to be back with family. But the stay was short, and I had no way of knowing that it would be the last time I would be with all of my immediate family members for many years.

A day or so after I was released, SNCC representatives approached me. Several SNCC members were making a fundraising trip to Kansas City and wanted me to accompany them. They felt that my story of attempting to buy a bus ticket and being incarcerated for twenty-eight days was an inspirational story and would be helpful in raising much-needed funds to continue the voter registration activities in McComb. With some reluctance, as I had just been reunited with my family, I agreed to go.

Except for short trips to Louisiana, it was the first time I had been out of the state of Mississippi. We were well-received at every stop. I was treated with celebrity status, something I had never sought and that made me somewhat uncomfortable. I am not by nature a shy person, but I am also not a person who seeks to promote myself or my achievements. But I understood my role. I realized I could be an inspiration to others, because at my young age, at great risk to myself, I had confronted one of the great evils in our society: racial segregation and discrimination. Mine was a story that needed to be told, and I was exhilarated by how well my friends and I were received.

However, the proverbial other shoe was about to fall.

OCTOBER 4, 1961, WAS a typical fall Mississippi day, hot but not as oppressively so as during the summer. On that morning, I readied myself for school, full of anticipation and excitement that I would be returning to school for my sophomore year after missing a full month of school due to my incarceration. My brother James and I boarded the bus, and on the ride I talked to many of my friends I had not seen since I was taken to jail. We talked about school, about the civil rights activities, and about what it was like to be in jail. My friends regarded me, as the people in Kansas City had, as a heroine.

We did talk a little about whether I anticipated any problems with registering for school, as everyone in the community knew what I had done, including my principal, Commodore Dewey Higgins. Principal Higgins had been the prime mover in black education in McComb and was responsible for getting the white school board to approve new buildings and improvements in the black schools—some of which I am sure were done to make our unequal educational system seem a bit more equal. White leaders feared that someday equal educational opportunity as mandated by *Brown v. Board of Education* might actually have to occur in Mississippi. In fact, integration did not actually arrive in McComb schools until 1965, when my younger sister, Marionette, was one of the first black students to attend the previously all-white high school. My friends and I were cognizant, even at our young ages, that Principal Higgins was beholden for his position to the white school board and the white community generally. We did not know how beholden, but we were soon to find out.

When I arrived at school, my brother and friends and I separated and I went to the school secretary's office to register for school. The secretary told me that I would have to see Principal Higgins. Shortly after, I was ushered into his office. Higgins was very cold and abrupt with me and told me that the school board had directed him to expel me.

Expelled! The words echoed through my ears. Here I was at age sixteen, having spent twenty-eight days in jail for standing up for our rights, and my principal would not stand up to the school board.

As I learned later, he even denied to the press that I had been expelled. He told the *McComb Enterprise-Journal* that Ike Lewis and I had been transferred to another school, a transfer allegedly arranged by SNCC. While my initial reaction was to be stunned, my anger soon arose and I said to Principal Higgins that I did not understand how he could let white folks run a colored school. I then got up and left, without a clear sense of where I was going or what I was going to do.

As I walked down the school hallway, some of my friends came up to me. Sensing by the look on my face that something was seriously wrong, they asked what had happened. I told them that Principal Higgins had expelled me. My friends became irate and began to talk about taking some action on my behalf. Others suggested since I had nowhere to go I should join them in the school assembly which was about to convene. At the same time, my friends started spreading the word throughout the school that I had been unjustly expelled and that some action would be taken. Talk began about a walkout from the school.

When we arrived at the assembly, Principal Higgins began addressing the students. I do not believe that he knew that I was present, or he might have had me physically removed. During the course of the assembly, one of the students, Joe Lewis, raised his hand and after being recognized asked Principal Higgins why Brenda Travis was not being allowed back in school. Rather than answer the question, the principal deflected it by telling Joe that he should come see him in his office after the assembly was over. This evasion further incensed the students.

When the assembly was over, many of the students did not leave the room, but rather called for a walkout to protest my expulsion. This was to be the first mass walkout of students at any all-black Mississippi school. I was exhilarated, triumphant, and felt vindicated by the actions of my fellow students. Students were encouraging other students to walk out with them. I approached my brother James, who told me that he could not walk out, as he had too much to risk being in his senior year, but that he was fully supportive of what the other students and I were doing. I loved my brother and respected his decision while disagreeing with it.

More than a hundred of us walked out, marching down the sidewalks in an orderly fashion. As with any unplanned but bold decisive action, we were filled with great emotion. I led the group and we all began to sing songs that some of us had learned at the nightly meetings at the Masonic Temple. As we passed an all-black elementary school along the way, I noticed one of the teachers watching with an approving look on her face as we paraded by. We were an incredible sight—a large group of high school students marching through the black community and singing freedom songs.

When we began the march, we had a vague sense that we would walk the nine miles to the county seat of Magnolia to present our grievances to the county officials. However, we went to the Masonic Temple first. As always at the Masonic Temple, there was a lot of activity going on. Jim Forman, executive secretary of SNCC, had decided to hold a staff meeting in McComb on October 4, so many SNCC workers were at the Temple when we arrived. Among them were Bob Moses; Chuck McDew, who at the time was SNCC chairman; and Robert Zellner, the first white SNCC field secretary, who had become involved in civil rights activities while a student at

Methodist-affiliated Huntingdon College in Montgomery, Alabama. Also at the Masonic temple were my friends, Hollis Watkins and Curtis Hayes, who had just recently been bailed out of jail with me.

There were so many of us that we could not all get into the Masonic Temple.

We told Bob, Chuck, and the others what had occurred and that we wanted to march to Magnolia or at least to the McComb City Hall. While Hollis and Curtis were enthusiastic and were immediately ready to join us, Bob and Chuck McDew expressed some reluctance, with Chuck suggesting that my suspension would likely be resolved within a few days and things would go back to normal. He also indicated that if our march went forward, opposition from white groups would only get worse and might further hamper attempts to get more of our parents registered to vote.

But Chuck and Bob's attempts to quell our youthful enthusiasm fell on deaf ears, and when they realized that we were a force that would not be stopped, they agreed to accompany us to City Hall.

While at the Masonic Temple, our group made up some poster boards and signs, some expressing outrage over my suspension, others demanding "Freedom Now." The McComb newspaper would later write that we had come to the Masonic Temple to pick up previously made signs, thus implying that our march was somehow pre-planned. In reality, of course, it was a spontaneous action by Burglund High School students who had been provoked by my expulsion.

When we left the Masonic Temple, Robert Zellner remained behind. This was on the recommendation of Moses and McDew, as both recognized that the presence of a white man within our black group would further infuriate the authorities and create a greater risk of violence, particularly for Zellner but also for the rest of us. However, when Zellner saw us leave, and more particularly when he heard our chorus of freedom songs, he was struck by our actions. Later, he recalled thinking of the quote from Gandhi: 'There go my people, I have to run and catch up because I am their leader." Heeding Gandhi's words, Zellner hurried out of the Masonic Temple and caught up with our group as we marched through the black community into the white community.

From the head of the march, I looked back at our troop train with great pride. Here we were, a group of young black people, high school students, marching down the streets in an organized, orderly manner. Our voices were loud, but loud in singing praises through the freedom songs that called out in unison. Neither McComb nor any other area of Mississippi had seen anything like the Burglund High School students.

As always, word quickly spread of our spontaneous activity. As we neared city hall, we could see in front of us the McComb city police as well as a large crowd of hostile white people. The hateful screams from those angry whites almost drowned out our impassioned singing. I am told that FBI agents were in the crowd observing what was going on and taking notes, but they did nothing to intervene in what was to follow.

As we neared the steps of city hall, a police officer called out over the din and told us to disperse, as we were an unlawful assembly. (The hostile white crowd was not similarly told to disperse.) My friend Hollis Watkins then ascended the steps of the city hall, indicating that he came to offer prayers as part of this peaceful assemblage. As he knelt to pray, an officer told him that he could not pray on the city hall steps, snatched him up, told him that he was under arrest, and moved him forcibly into the city hall. I then stepped forward, following Hollis's lead, and knelt at the top of the stairs and began to pray. I was terrified, then I was grabbed so violently by a police officer that I was pulled right out of my shoes. I was forcibly escorted barefooted into the city hall and down the stairs into the police lockup.

A number of my fellow students followed my lead and when one of my friends, Janie Campbell, saw my plight, she gave me her shoes.

While a large number of us were being penned like cattle in the bowels of city hall, high drama was going on outside. The crowd of white folks began to move in on the demonstrators, focusing their attention on the older members of the group, Bob Moses and Chuck McDew, and most particularly on Bob Zellner. As Moses and McDew feared, the white crowd was most deeply incensed by the presence of a white person with our group. By chance, one of the members of the white mob had attended the same college as Zellner in Montgomery and recognized him.

The threats against Zellner then became more ominous and personal, as the crowd moved toward him and some of the whites began to beat him and try to pull him away from our group. The beating that Zellner took was savage; he tried to hold onto the metal handrail of the city hall steps to keep himself somewhat upright and prevent being pulled into the white crowd. Bob Moses and Chuck McDew also took beatings as they tried to intervene to prevent Zellner from being killed. As Zellner held tight to the handrail with Moses and McDew in turn hanging onto him, an older white man came up to Zellner, grabbed him by his head, and attempted to gouge out his eyes.

The police, as they had with the Freedom Riders in Birmingham and Montgomery, let the mob have its way for a while before they finally intervened. And their intervention was to arrest Moses, McDew, and Zellner, while taking no action whatsoever against the mob that had assaulted Zellner and company.

Well over a hundred of us were now in custody, crowded into a lockup that was designed for less than fifty. Some of my friends were nervous, having come from "good" homes and never expecting that they would end up in jail. At sixteen, being an experienced hand at jail, or so I thought at the time, I reassured them that what we were doing was the right thing, and that we had nothing to fear, as we were together in this venture and what we were doing collectively was bigger than any of us individually.

During the entire time we were in the lockup, we were all forced to stand, as there was literally no room to sit. We were like cattle or hogs waiting to be slaughtered, a thought that unhappily ran through the minds of my friends and fellow students.

Then one after another of us, including Hollis Watkins, would be taken out to be interrogated. Soon parents began to arrive at the City Hall. Many of the parents were supportive of what their children had done. However, others parents were very angry, berated their children, and after obtaining their release physically beat them in the view of the rest of us, who could only cry out for our friends, as we remained behind bars.

The parents who beat their children were later praised by the authorities as well as by the local newspaper which wrote an editorial on the day following our walkout. It expressed a biased view of what was transpiring in McComb and vicinity during these early days of the civil rights movement. The editorial, written by Oliver Emmerich, entitled "Adult Negros Should Use Parental Authority," read as follows:

> It is obvious that our Negro people are being misled in McComb.
>
> Schools are developed for the purpose of providing educational facilities for children. It is senseless to permit agitators to enter our schools and use them for any other purpose.
>
> That scene at City Hall yesterday can serve no good purpose whatsoever. And sensible Negro people know it.
>
> Our Negro schools are modern. Our Negro teachers are

paid the same wages as white teachers. Our Negro children are transported in modern buses.

Every effort has been made by our school authorities to provide the maximum in school advantages to our Negro people. The proposition of voting does not enter the school situation in any way whatsoever.

If a Negro wants to vote and is qualified he will not be turned down by Chancery Clerk Wendell Holmes, who is conscientiously trying to uphold the law. Some of our Negro people have been voting for many years in Pike County.

What is happening to our community when children march on City Hall under the leadership of outside agitators?

It's time that our adult Negroes use some paternal authority. The Negro people will accomplish nothing by resorting to such childlike tactics.

We hold that our adult Negroes should accept their responsibilities in this matter and not permit teenagers and agitators to create a situation which could seriously damage the best interests of all our people.

I quote this editorial in its entirety as it reflects in many ways the "moderate" white view of race relations in McComb as of 1961. However, the editorial is full of untruths. It does not state that the registrar was not registering every black person who presented him or herself. The registrar initially had registered black applicants but stopped doing so after this very newspaper alerted the white community as to what was evolving in the black community.

Further, we young people who chose to act on our rights did so not because we were led by outsiders, but because we knew that the system that we lived under was unjust and if we did not speak out, no one would. Indeed at times the outsiders attempted to discourage us from taking action for fear we would be hurt or that we would escalate tensions such that other civil rights activities would be impeded.

Oftentimes, we the people were leading our leaders and not vice versa, as well as it should be.

ON THAT SAME EVENING as I watched my friends being released, who were wishing me well, there was another arrest. My mentor, C. C. Bryant, was arrested at his home, allegedly for contributing to the delinquency of minors, when in fact he played no role in the Burglund High School walkout.

As the lockup began to clear out, and I began to ponder my ultimate fate, the police came to get me and the SNCC activists, including Hollis and Curtis. Again we were taken to Magnolia to be housed in the Pike County jail. Again I was the only woman incarcerated and was transported by myself to Magnolia and put back in the same cell from which I had just recently been released.

This time I was not prepared. I did not have even a change of underwear and was wearing my friend Janie Campbell's shoes. No one told me what was going to happen to me or what I was charged with, if indeed I was charged with any crime. I had just witnessed the astounding hate-fueled rage of the white mob. Bob, Chuck, and Bob Zellner had been brutally beaten. I had watched black parents, no doubt acting out of fear of the whites, beating their own children as punishment for taking a civil rights stand.

I was terrified.

8

The Reformatory

As it turned out, my second stay in Magnolia was very short. The next morning, after spending the night in the Pike County jail, I was escorted in handcuffs out of the jail by police officers and placed into the back of a patrol car. I was not taken before a judge, nor did the officers tell me where we were going. In what one author has called the cruelest sentence of all, I soon found out that my destination was the Oakley reformatory for "delinquent Negro youth" in Raymond, Mississippi. For seeking service at a bus station and for attempting to pray on the steps of City Hall, I was to be exiled to a facility for young women who had been involved in criminal activity. When I arrived at this facility—segregated, as were all Mississippi facilities—I was told by the superintendent that I would likely remain there until I was twenty-one. I faced the loss of five years of my life.

While I pondered my fate and life behind bars in a different kind of jail, a different set of events was taking place in McComb with my fellow activists and my brothers and sisters who had walked out with me from Burglund High School. The SNCC activists were soon bailed out of jail, with a trial scheduled for late October. Meanwhile, my fellow students soon faced the harsh reality and results of their actions. With the same vindictiveness that Principal Higgins had expelled me from school, he announced to the walk-out students that if they wanted to return to school, they would have to sign a pledge that they would no longer be involved in any demonstrations. Principal Higgins was doing the bidding of his white masters.

As might be expected, some parents and some students acquiesced. I am proud to say that more did not. For several days after the walkout, these students would show up for school, put their books on their desks, and walk out. This took place until Principal Higgins issued an ultimatum that the students return to school by October 16 and sign the pledge to no longer demonstrate, or be expelled. Close to a hundred of my fellow students chose the same fate that Principal Higgins had bestowed upon me—they were expelled.

Bob Moses and the SNCC activists were concerned about the large number of expelled students and felt that something needed to be done to prevent the loss of their educational opportunities because they had the courage to exercise their rights. They came up with the concept of "Nonviolent High," an alternative school taught by the SNCC activists. A number of the SNCC folk who were college-educated—likely better educated than some of the teachers at our school—assigned the tasks for the various school subjects. Bob Moses, who had been a math teacher at one of the best public schools in New York City, became the math teacher at the makeshift school. Chuck McDew, whose initial baptism into the civil rights movement was at South Carolina State College, became the history teacher. Chemistry and physics were taught by Dion Diamond, who earlier that year had been a Freedom Rider attempting to desegregate the buses and bus terminals in Jackson and was jailed for his efforts.

Although I do not think that Bob recognized it at the time, what he set up in McComb in the fall of 1961 was the prototype for the "Freedom Schools" that would be set up across Mississippi during the 1964 Freedom Summer project. Interestingly, Chuck would later relate that in the course of working with the walk-out students in McComb, he was amazed at how indoctrinated they had been into the overall construct of white supremacy. Burglund High was an all-black school, but its curriculum and its teachers were answerable to the white segregationists who ran the schools and everything else in Mississippi. He recalled, for instance, that during a discussion about the Civil War, one of the students referred to it as the "War for Southern Independence."

"Nonviolent High" in 1961 and the Freedom Schools in 1964 were a breath of fresh air into the stale atmosphere of Mississippi's segregated educational system.

MEANWHILE, I WAS NOT enjoying the same benefits of schooling after expulsion as my classmates. While Oakley was euphemistically called a "reform" school, little was done to reform anyone, and in any case I had done nothing to be reformed from. Essentially we were housed as in any other jail setting, although we slept in dormitories, not individual cells. The only education that any of us received was a home economics class, which apparently was the only thing that the authorities thought black girls should be prepared for. I welcomed the class as a diversion from the lack of other activities, and I helped set up a baseball team so that there would be something else we could do to get through the day.

One other diversion was that on Sunday we were allowed to go to church in a nearby community. Those of us who chose to go were put on a bus and driven to the church. We were required to sit together during the service, and when it was over, we had to re-board the bus to go back to Oakley. On the return trip, the bus would stop at a store where we were allowed to purchase small items, if we had money. During the trips to and from church, we were relatively free, but no one ever ventured to run or escape, as we were in very rural counties and there was no place to run to.

Needless to say, I was the only "delinquent" who was incarcerated for civil rights activities. For the first several weeks I was in Oakley, my mother had no idea where I was, as the authorities would tell her nothing. She feared that I had met the fate of other blacks such as Emmett Till. During this time, my mother was also forced to relocate to find work to care for the family. Initially, she went to the Mississippi Gulf Coast to work at a hotel, and later she went to Jackson, always sending her meager earnings back to the family in McComb. She obtained employment in Jackson through the assistance of Jack Young, the lawyer who represented me when I was initially imprisoned because of the events at the McComb Greyhound bus station. Young was one of the few black lawyers in Mississippi at the time. It took great courage to represent civil rights workers and locals like me who had become involved in civil rights issues.

I am told that on one occasion during my long stay at Oakley, my mother and a group of others (mostly students from McComb) tried to visit me. Fred Bates, a black entrepreneur who operated his own service station in McComb and also was an independent bus driver, arranged for a busload of people to come to Oakley to visit me, unbeknownst to me. They set out for the school, but when they arrived and inquired about seeing me, they were provided no information—not even whether I was actually in the facility. When they did not immediately leave, reform school authorities with snarling dogs drove them away from the facility. The commotion from the yelling and the snarling dogs caused me and the other Oakley residents to wonder what was taking place outside our gated community, but I did not know until later that the commotion was related to my family and friends just trying to visit me.

Later that day, I asked one of the matrons about the bus that was driven away from the facility. The matron did not know anything, but a short while later, I was summoned to the superintendent's office. I knew that this could not be good news. The superintendent matter-of-factly told me that the bus had contained my friends and family, and that he had turned the bus away because the group had not sought permission to visit me. It's hard to explain the anger that I felt at knowing that my life was so controlled by others that I could be deprived of the simple right to have a visit from my mother and friends.

I became enraged, forgetting for the moment that I was in prison, had been for months, and I was now in the office of the person who ran the facility. I started yelling uncontrollably at the superintendent. He said that if I did not stop talking to him in that way he would slap me. I don't know what possessed me, but I responded that if he dared lift a hand at me, there would be all-out war. I was not thinking at this time about my training in nonviolence, but only about the audacity of this man to turn away my family that I longed to see. The superintendent did not strike me, but rather called for a matron to escort me out. I seethed for days afterwards.

After my mother found work in Jackson, she made arrangements through the facility to come and see me. She was not turned away. I never knew how she made such arrangements because she had no car, but I believe that someone in the movement helped her to get to Oakley. Her visits were a godsend. We would hug each other and talk about her life, the family, and what was going on in the movement in McComb. Although she had little and earned little, she would always bring me things, including clothes, food, and money. While our visits were necessarily short, my mother always told me that she was proud of me for what I had done and that she knew that with the help of God, I would persevere in this trial that I was going through.

There have been times in my life when I have marveled at my own resiliency, my ability to survive and even thrive under adverse conditions, and Oakley Negro Juvenile Reformatory was one of these situations. I was fortunate, as I have been fortunate at other times in my life, to have had someone look out for me. At Oakley it was the matron of the facility, Mary Turner. Mama Turner, as I called her, truly became my surrogate mother. Except for her, I was completely alone during my time in the reformatory school, with no one else to offer support. After I learned that I had been denied a visit from my mother, I gave up. I realized that they had taken everything from me—my freedom, my family, and my own mother—and, as a sixteen-year-old child, I couldn't think of anything worth living for.

But Mama Turner took me under her wing and encouraged me to stay focused and true to myself and never, ever to stop believing in myself. She and her husband would, at times, bring me out of the dormitory at night just to talk to me and even give me a little extra food. To my sixteen-year-old self at the time, Mama Turner seemed "old," as all people older than themselves seem to teenagers. But she was a saint, a very dear person who believed in my innate goodness and offered me love, kindness, and caring in a situation that was not designed to offer those comforts. I will forever be grateful for the actions and love expressed to me by Mama Turner.

WHILE I LINGERED IN Oakley facing five years of banishment from my family and community, the whites in McComb took every opportunity to snuff out the nascent civil rights revolution that was going on in the community. In mid-October, two out-of-state observers came to McComb. The two, Paul Potter of the National Student Association and Tom Hayden of the Students for a Democratic Society, had a rude introduction to Mississippi. Both were dragged in broad daylight from the car they were driving and were brutally beaten in the streets of McComb.

The SNCC activists, who had remained out of jail on bail and who were teaching the students at Nonviolent High, met a fate similar to my own in front of the same judge who had originally sentenced me (and was likely the person responsible for sending me to Oakley). On October 31, Bob Moses, Chuck McDew, Bob Zellner, and other activists, including the older Burglund High School students, were convicted of disturbing the peace and given prison sentences ranging from four to six months in the county jail. After sentencing the men and women—including my friend Janie Campbell, who had lent me her shoes at the city hall—Judge Brumfield told them as they were led off to jail: "Some of you are local residents, some of you are outsiders. Those of you who are local residents are like sheep being led to the slaughter." Brumfield's words echoed his statements to me when I appeared before him— he could not fathom how young "colored" residents of McComb could have acted on our own to rise up against the tyranny that was oppressing us.

Just as I had found unlikely comfort through Mama Turner at Oakley, the SNCC and local activists found some comfort while waiting in the county jail for funds to be raised to bail them out. People from McComb reached out to the imprisoned activists, visiting them and bringing them extra food, some of it cooked by the fearless Aylene Quin at her cafe. Bobby Talbert is quoted as saying that the food was so good that he gained twenty-five pounds while incarcerated. The locals also brought books and other materials including paper and pens. Bob Moses was able to write and smuggle out an inspiring and hopeful note:

> We are smuggling this note from the drunk tank of the county jail in Magnolia, Mississippi. Twelve of us are here, sprawled along the concrete bunker; Curtis Hayes, Hollis Watkins, Ike Lewis, and Robert Talbert, four veterans of the bunker, are sitting up talking—mostly about girls; Charles McDew ("Tell the Story") is curled into the concrete and the wall; Harold Robinson, Stephen

Ashley, James Wells, Lee Chester Vick, Leotus Eubanks and
Ivory Diggs lay camped on the cold bunker; I am sitting with
smuggled pen and paper, thinking a little, writing a little. . . .
Myrtis Bennett and Janie Campbell are across the way wedded
to a different icy cubicle. . . . This is Mississippi, the middle of
the iceberg. Hollis is leading off with his tenor, "Michael, row
the boat ashore, Alleluia; Christian brothers don't be slow, Alleluia; Mississippi's next to go, Alleluia." This is a tremor in the
middle of the iceberg—from a stone that the builders rejected.

However, the positive tone of Bob's note did not reflect what
was going on in the greater McComb community. Violence against
civil rights activists was the white community's typical response to
protests of any kind. In early November, after the Interstate Com-
merce Commission issued a ruling prohibiting segregation in bus
terminals, members of the Congress of Racial Equality (CORE)
tried to test the ruling by seeking service at the food counter in the
McComb Greyhound terminal. When the CORE representatives
entered the terminal, they were cursed and then attacked by whites.
FBI agents were present but merely took notes and did nothing
to stem the violence. After letting whites have their way with the
CORE activists for five minutes, the local police arrived to break
up the attack, even though most of the damage was already done.
Later in November, a shotgun blast was fired into a home occupied
by SNCC workers. In December, out-of-town newspapermen were
attacked, as were three more CORE people at the bus station.

Amidst all this accelerating activity on the outside, time was
passing very slowly for me inside the Oakley Negro Juvenile Reformatory. Boredom is a constant companion for the incarcerated. Days
and weeks went by monotonously. At age sixteen, I contemplated a
long-term incarceration. What made my incarceration even more

difficult is that I was totally separated from all that I held dear: my immediate family and my civil rights family. Most of my "brothers" in the movement—and most of them were brothers—had the companionship of other activists, as Bob Moses so poignantly wrote in his missive from the Pike County Jail. As the only incarcerated female, I did not have such camaraderie to lift my spirits, to be reminded daily that others just like me were joined in sacrifice for a cause. This loneliness, this separation, weighed on me at times, and I would try to focus on the mundane activities of my captivity so that the pain and loss would not overwhelm me. It was a struggle, and I would often have to remind myself that what I was enduring was for a greater good. This would have been a challenge for anyone, let alone a sixteen-year-old.

My seventeenth birthday in March 1962 came and went without notice. There was no card, no cake, nothing to commemorate what would have been a festive day had I been home with my family.

Easter Sunday 1962 arrived similarly like any other day, but it was not to be like any other day. As I celebrated within myself the resurrection of our Savior, little did I know that I was going to be "saved" from one form of prison that very day. Buried in my thoughts, I barely noticed Mama Turner approaching me with a smile on her face. She awoke me from my thoughts by announcing that there were important visitors to see me and that I needed to bring my belongings to the superintendent's office immediately.

"Important visitors?" I said incredulously. "I don't get visitors, other than my mother." I kept thinking somehow it was my mother, who my heart longed to see.

"Hurry," Mama Turner said.

When I arrived at the superintendent's office, there were a number of people in the office, including a middle-aged white man and two young black women about my age. The middle-aged white man, introduced himself, with a heavy accent, as Professor

Paul Fischer* of Talladega College in Alabama. He introduced the young women who were with him as students at the college.

Sensing my discomfort, Professor Fischer explained that he had heard about my situation. SNCC representatives, unbeknownst to me, had broadcast my story, and it had been published in newspapers and magazines throughout the United States. Being a refugee himself from Germany, my story had resonated with him, and he had resolved to do something to help me. Although he did not go into all the details to me of how he was able to negotiate my freedom, he did explain that he had spoken with Mississippi Governor Ross Barnett, who had agreed to release me from Oakley on the condition that I leave the state within twenty-four hours, never to return.

My head was spinning. My imprisonment was soon to be over, but I would be exiled from my state, my family, and friends.

I was highly suspicious and would never have left the facility with this white man only, but I was relieved and comforted by the presence of the two black students with him. He must have known this.

I was saved. On resurrection day.

I hugged and kissed Mama Turner, and soon the professor, the students, and I left Oakley. I was going to a new life, far from my home, but I knew it was the price necessary to pay for my activism.

As we drove away from Oakley, I looked back one last time, unaware that the savior with whom I was leaving was no better, in fact was worse, than the judge, the police, and the white residents of McComb put together. My salvation was a sham.

---

* Not his real name.

9

A Devil in Disguise

As we left Oakley, I told Professor Fischer and the young women that before I departed Mississippi, I had to see my mother one last time. If I was being banished from my home state, I could not leave without a goodbye to my mother who had stood beside me in my darkest hours and had suffered greatly, all because I had chosen to fight for my freedom and hers. The professor agreed, and as I learned when we arrived at the home where my mother was renting a room in Jackson, he and other members of the movement had planned all along for me to visit my mom. Indeed, someone, probably from SNCC, had learned of my imminent release and arranged for *Jet* magazine's photographer to be at my mom's when I arrived.

What a joyous, bittersweet reunion we had! Our time together was short but filled with hugs, kisses, laughter, and tears. I had grown a lot since that fateful day in August 1961 when I volunteered to integrate the Greyhound bus station. I was now seventeen, and despite the difficult circumstances that I had encountered over the last nine months—jail, expulsion, jail, and then the reformatory—I had survived. And now, for a few precious moments, I was with the one person who was always there for me, the one person who most cared about me in life, and from whom I was about to be separated again.

The time with my mother raced by. I do remember one aspect

of that short visit. Others who knew of my release, and knew that I would have to be uprooted again and leave Mississippi, wanted to give me a sendoff. Webb "Doc" Owens, who along with C. C. Bryant had led the civil rights activities in McComb, brought me a gift, a brightly colored parasol. While it was a small gesture, it meant a lot to me, as it let me know that people cared and appreciated what I had done.

And then it was time to go, as we needed to be out of Mississippi within twenty-four hours and the clock was ticking. There was one last goodbye and then we climbed into the professor's vehicle and were on our way to Talladega.

Most of the conversation on the long ride to Talladega was between me and the two young women who had accompanied the professor. We bonded and the bond would continue during my stay in Talladega. To these college students, I was a wonder. I had done what many blacks dreamed of doing, but fear prevented them from doing. I had stood up to the system. Not only had I stood up to the system, I had gone to jail and spent many months in captivity. They plied me with questions and I answered as best as I could, as I was caught up in a whirlwind, not knowing what would happen next.

When we arrived in Talladega, we went immediately to the professor's home on campus. As we entered, he told me that this was now going to be my home and that I was a part of his family. He introduced me to his wife and two sons—Frank, who was in his twenties, and Mario, fourteen. I sensed a lack of warmth in their greetings, a sense that would remain with me during my entire time in Talladega. My new "home" was so unlike our five-room house in McComb. This house had electricity, running water, and toilets. For the first time in life, I was to have a bedroom all to myself.

Yet my instincts told me something was amiss. I did not know at the time what was making me uncomfortable, and as I fell asleep that first night in my very own bed, I thought that perhaps I was just feeling the newness, the strangeness, of being far away from my real home and being with white folks for the first time in my life. I slept soundly, if warily.

From the beginning of my stay in Talladega, the professor was effusive in how he spoke about me and to me. He called me his "daughter," the daughter that he always wanted and now had. When he returned each night from his teaching regimen, I was the first person he greeted, always in glowing and gushing terms. He began to profess his love to me. He always referred to me as his daughter, but again my senses were telling me that something wasn't quite right. I never knew a father, so I was at a loss as to how to react to this man who fawned all over me. Certainly I had known some important adult male figures, but the professor's manner toward me was far different from anything that I had ever experienced. While I had always longed for a loving, caring father, something wasn't right about how this man was interacting with me, but I just didn't know what it was.

And then it started. A touch here, a pat on the back, a kiss or a hug that lasted too long. The professor always wanted to be near me, to be in close physical proximity. And while I wasn't sure what was going on, as I suspect any abused person is unaware initially, I knew somehow that the pats and the touches and the statements about "his beautiful daughter" were not right. But I did not know where to turn or what to do.

It was late April when I was released from Oakley, so it was too late for me to enroll in school in Talladega. I would spend my days either at home or I would go to the college dormitory to talk to the two young women who had been with me when I was released from Oakley. Our bond grew stronger. We would talk for long hours, about girl stuff, boys, and school. We would go together to downtown Talladega, a small city in east central Alabama, about one and a half times as large as McComb. Talladega was home not only to the historically black Talladega College but also to a large state-run school for the deaf and blind (actually two parallel segregated programs at the time; they merged in 1968).

I was most comfortable when I was with these young women. Even though I had not finished high school, they treated me as their equal or even sometimes, because of my civil rights notoriety, as special. The most pleasant parts of my stay in Talladega were when I was with these young women, away from the brooding sense of dread that would come over me when I had to return to the professor's house.

From August 1961 through April 1962, I had led the life of an exile, but my spirits always remained high. Despite the separation from my family, I remained strong, believing that I was part of something much bigger than myself and that some suffering was a necessary part of what it would take to accomplish meaningful change. But now, though liberated from one prison, I felt like I was suffocating in another. I began to feel depressed, lonely, and lost. I felt like a victim, which I indeed was, but a helpless and hopeless one. I was feeling sorry for myself and my fate, feelings I never had before. Prayer was my solace in the midst of this perverted wasteland, and only prayer comforted me.

IN THE MIDST OF this enervating malaise, some positive things happened, although when the positive moment would pass, the depression would return. The first of these positive occurrences was a result of something that had taken place while I was in Oakley. A social worker recognized my talents and heard about a contest through a sorority. She recommended that I write a story and submit it for consideration. I wasn't sure what to write about, but since I had been a member of a 4-H club, I remembered that when I was young in McComb, I volunteered through the 4-H club to accept fifty Rhode Island Red chicks to care for. So I wrote a story about my experiences having the primary responsibility for raising the chickens. While Mama Turner and the others at Oakley believed in me, I turned in my story without any expectations. Later, after I was in Talladega, how surprised I was to find out that I had won a prize for my story and would be presented with an award in New York City! The award was to be presented by the Louis Weintraub Foundation. My expenses and those of a chaperone would be paid for the trip to New York.

My chaperone turned out to be Aurelia Young, wife of my attorney, Jack Young. Mrs. Young would look out for me on this trip and in the years that would follow, another of my many mother figures in life. Mrs. Young and I flew to New York together. I have no recollection of what airport we flew out of, but I enjoyed my first airplane flight. We stayed at the renowned Waldolf-Astoria Hotel and were feted during our short stay in New York.

But even in this wonderful moment, the dark cloud clung to me. My savior, Professor Fischer, insisted on going to New York to accompany me and Mrs. Young. The shadow of his presence was dominating, and I thought of reaching out to Mrs. Young, but my own fear kept me from doing so. While in New York, the professor wrote me notes—in essence love letters—that made me cringe, even though he always called me "his beloved daughter." Here is an excerpt from one of the many notes that he wrote me:

> Because I love you so much. As my new daughter, as my co-fighter for freedom and human dignity and as my young friend. You know, you must know that a daughter I selected means more than a natural daughter, although I love my own daughter very, very much. I loved you before I saw you for the very first time. I loved you for your courage, for what you have done, because

you suffered such injustice being still so young.

You are so many things to me: daughter, co-freedom fighter, young friend, beauty, charm, my private student, consolation and human being who, as young as you are, understands me and my problem.

As long as I know you are with us, I may have, I feel, the strength to find a solution to my problem. You mean new hope to me. Without you, my life may end now. Your presence makes me so happy.

Those words and others that the professor wrote me still unnerve me fifty-plus years later. I had left a state which was the consummate symbol of evil, only to fall into the hands of a savior who truly had the devil inside.

I did reach out once to Mrs. Fischer. I told her what was taking place between her husband and me, the notes and letters, the unwanted kisses, hugs and touches. I think she knew what was going on and just looked the other way. When I finally had the courage to reach out to her, she rebuffed me, telling me that there was nothing that she could do, as she was Jewish and the professor, a German native, had rescued her from sure death at the hands of the Nazi regime. Because she was forever indebted to him, she was helpless to do anything to help me. One who was rescued could not reach out to rescue another. My depression continued.

Although many years have gone by since I was subjected to Professor Fischer's abuse, it is still difficult to think about or to express. Perhaps, sadly, the only person who can fully understand what I felt and what I went through is someone who experienced similar abuse. A range of emotions describe what I felt and what I feel today as I write these words. Shame. Hurt. Responsibility. Anger. Distrust. Powerlessness. As victims often do, I felt that I was somehow to blame for having brought this on.

My situation was even more complex because there was a race factor in my abuse, combined with the unique situation that I found myself in. Here was a white man, a much older white man, coming on to me, as many white men in plantation times and later had come on to young, or not so young, helpless black women. Many black women over the years were forced to submit, but I vowed that I never would, even though my situation seemed so helpless and hopeless. While many of my black and white sisters know that no one will believe them if they try to report the abuse, even in this my situation differed, as the person I tried to report my abuse to knew that what I was saying was true, but she did nothing to help me. I was caught up in a story that would rival anything that horror movie or book writers could invent. There seemed to be no solution.

WHEN THE SCHOOL YEAR at Talladega College ended in the spring of 1962, Professor Fischer took a summer teaching position at Atlanta University. He insisted that I accompany him on his weekly trips to Atlanta. We would leave on Monday mornings and return late on Fridays. Sometimes on our drives, particularly on our return trips on Friday, he would pull off the highway and say he just wanted to be with me, just the two of us. He would put his hands between my legs, and when I would try to push his hands away, he would just smile at me and tell me how much he loved me.

Fortunately, Atlanta University provided housing for the professor, and he had arranged for me to stay in a room in the house of a lovely woman, Mrs. Brown. However, at the end of every day, he would insist that we have dinner together at Paschal's Restaurant, famously frequented over the years by civil rights activists and politicians in Atlanta.

There was also a bright spot in the Atlanta trips. Because I had nothing to do in Atlanta, I went down to the SNCC offices. The

SNCC headquarters were in Atlanta, and because I knew and had worked with many SNCC activists in McComb, I was welcomed at the Atlanta offices. I met Jim Forman, then the executive secretary of SNCC, Julian Bond, Mary King, and many others.

I would do whatever I could to help out at the office, including secretarial work. It made me feel like I was part of the movement again. It also liberated my thoughts and feelings and gave me something creative and positive to put my energies into.

I became friends with many of the SNCC workers, particularly Jim Forman. After a while, I felt that I could let down my guard, and I approached Jim to tell him what I was going through at the hands of my savior. I showed him one of the notes in which the professor had written how beautiful I was and compared me to a Sphinx. The ever irrepressible Jim Forman called the professor a dirty, rotten SOB. He said he was prepared to help me and that I could reach out to him at any time. I thanked him, but I was too fearful to take Jim up on his offer at that time, fearing that if I left the professor, I would be sent back to Mississippi and Oakley. However, I kept Jim's offer in the back of my mind.

UP TO THIS TIME, while the professor had hugged and kissed me and been intimate with me in ways that are too painful to describe, he had never tried to rape me. But on one of the weekends back in Talladega, he came on to me. Instinctively, I knew he intended to do more than just hug and caress me. Even though I had rebuffed many of his previous advances merely by pushing him away, I knew this time that he was far more serious than he had ever been and that I had to deal with this devilish fiend once and for all. As he tried to corral me, with all of the strength that I had, I took my left hand and hit him as hard as I could. God, coupled with my adrenaline, must have been on my side as I knocked him across the room. I did not think. I knew I had to flee. I ran past the fallen professor and out the door. I had nothing except the clothes on my back.

I ran down the street. I had no plan or place to go, but I knew I had to escape and that once the professor collected himself, he would be after me. Oh, the stories I imagined he would tell. For having rescued me and taken me into his home and cared for me, what I had done—I had assaulted him. And who would believe a young, black woman whose accuser in segregated Alabama was a distinguished, white professor. I had nowhere to go and nowhere to turn.

However, as I ran I came to the home of another Talladega professor, a black man whose son I had met while at Talladega. The son and I had talked about attending high school together in the fall, as we were about the same age. In fear and trembling, I knocked on the professor's door. He answered and took me in, obviously noting how emotional I was. Although I probably should have been concerned that this professor, as a colleague of Professor Fischer, would turn me back over to him, he did not.

He listened to me intently and seemed both understanding and sympathetic. When I had blurted out my entire story, he asked what I wanted to do. My first and only thought was to reach out to Jim Forman in Atlanta, who had agreed to help me out when I needed it. I asked him to call Jim, which he did. Jim calmed me and assured me. He asked that the professor come back on the phone, and he told the professor to take me immediately to the bus station and buy me a one-way ticket to Atlanta. He assured the professor that he would reimburse him for the cost of the ticket. He told the professor to stay with me at the bus station until I was on the bus, and then to call Jim with the time when I would be arriving in Atlanta, as Jim would meet me at the bus station.

As we left for the bus station, I was relieved but could not help feeling that I was being exiled again.

The bus ride from Talladega to Atlanta seemed to take forever.

I was alone again as I had been in prison and at Oakley, but there was also an element of fear. I kept imagining the professor coming after me. I knew that he would not let what I had done go unaddressed. However, I also knew that I was going to a truly safe place because I knew and trusted Jim Forman.

Much to my relief, the bus arrived in Atlanta, and there at the bus station were Jim and his wife, Mildred. They greeted me warmly, with hugs, and told me that I was safe with them. My anxiety level was still very high as I left the bus station with the Formans. I even looked around as we left, feeling that somehow my savior/devil might be right behind me. My instincts were correct, as they often are.

When we arrived at the Formans' home, the three of us sat around and talked. I told the Formans exactly what happened. Jim and Mildred did everything to comfort me and assure me that I was safe with them.

And then there was a knock at the door.

Jim got up to answer the door, proceeding cautiously as it was late at night and as the head of SNCC he had been the subject of many attacks and death threats. For reasons that are unclear to me now, I followed Jim as he walked to the door, and Jim's wife followed behind, boxing me in. Jim called out, as the knocking continued, and a voice responded that it was the police. A shudder ran down my spine. Jim, continuing to proceed with caution, began to open the door a crack, knowing that the police were often the enemy and that we might all be at risk. He opened the door to two white police officers, accompanied by Professor Fischer. The look on Fischer's face was one of sheer hatred, as he blurted out, "There she is. She is a fugitive from justice. Arrest her and she needs to be sent back to Mississippi."

My anxiety turned to utter terror. I imagined being led off in handcuffs to be sent back to prison in Mississippi, this time not because of exercising my constitutional rights, but because I had exercised my right to be free from abuse, an abuse that many black women had been subjected to. Jim placed himself between the police, Professor Fischer, and me, and I was grateful for the force of Jim's character. But I still felt doomed, as it would be my word as a young black woman against that of a white professor. Fischer kept interrupting Jim and the officers, saying that I was an escapee from a juvenile facility and that I should be arrested. The officers persuaded Jim to let them talk to me privately.

When the officers began talking to me, they asked my birthdate and I told them that I had turned seventeen in March. They suddenly left and went back to where Jim and Fischer were squared off. They said that because I was seventeen, I was an emancipated adult by Georgia standards, and as an emancipated adult, I was not subject to being returned to a juvenile facility in Mississippi.

Professor Fischer kept ranting that I was a fugitive, but the police told him that legally there was nothing they could do to make me go with them. They left, and I broke into tears as the Formans hugged me and assured me that my ordeal was over, all because I had turned seventeen. It was another amazing twist in the journey that had begun some nine or ten months before.

10

The Wandering

After my escape from the clutches of the devil, I stayed with the Formans for a short time. They then arranged for another place for me to stay. Julian Bond's sister, Jane, owned a home that she did not live in. She opened up the home to me and another SNCC worker, Sheila, whose last name I have forgotten. But before I moved into the home, another SNCC worker, Martha Prescod, invited me to go with her on a visit to her hometown, Detroit, Michigan, as a sort of R & R, to get away from the turmoil that was besieging me and to help me forget some of the traumatic events in my life. Although the trip was only a week's duration, it was good to be out of the South and its restrictive race policies and to be somewhere free at least of the open hostility that was ever-present in Mississippi, Alabama, and Georgia.

When I returned from Detroit, I moved in with Sheila in Jane's home. Shortly afterwards, my SNCC friends did another wonderful thing for me. They arranged for my mother to take the bus from Jackson to Atlanta to stay with me for a week. I cannot express how grateful I am for the kindness of the SNCC people. They knew my anguish and knew that there was only one person, my mom, who could offer the inner comfort and warmth that was missing in my life. Mom and I explored Atlanta, or as much as we could, as she made very little money and I made even less. The week flew by and then Mom was gone, leaving me with only my SNCC family to count on.

For that summer of 1962, I spent most of my days at the SNCC offices doing whatever I could to help out—typing, answering the phone, sealing envelopes, and just generally hanging out with the wonderfully brave people who worked for SNCC. There I met many SNCC veterans who have remained friends for life. I would often attend meetings where SNCC strategies and projects would be discussed at great length. Much to my surprise, at a number of these open meetings, my abuser nemesis, Professor Fischer, would appear. I marveled at his audacity to show up at events where I would likely appear; he knew that at least some of the SNCC workers were aware of what he had done and tried to do to me. When I would steal a glance at him, his face always seemed angrily contorted, reflecting the essence of the most evil person I ever encountered, more evil than the segregationists who had enslaved me.

At one of the SNCC conferences, I met the woman who was to become my next mother figure: Ella Baker. I affectionately called her "Ma Baker." Mrs. Baker was one of the many heroes of the civil rights movement who were often overlooked because they did their important work in the background while others were in the headlines. She was an activist and journalist in the 1930s, was a staff member and organizer for the NAACP from 1938 to 1953, and went to work in Atlanta for the Southern Christian Leadership Conference soon after it formed in 1957. Almost single-handedly, she brought together the sit-in students from across the South at the April 1960 Shaw University conference from which SNCC was formed. In her great wisdom, she convinced the students to form their own organization outside the influence and control of the more staid organizations such as the NAACP and SCLC. Without her, SNCC would not have existed, and without SNCC, the civil rights movement would not have taken the course that it did.

But for me personally, Ma Baker was to be a mother, friend,

and guide. She recognized my anguish and took me under her wing, talking to me, working with me. Jim Forman had told her what I had been through. She comforted me, assuring me of my goodness as a person. She recognized that I needed to complete my schooling, which I had promised my mother that I would do. I had lost my whole sophomore year of high school because of my stay in jail and then my imprisonment at Oakley.

Mrs. Baker had contacts throughout the South and reached out to a private school in North Carolina, where she had grown up, and arranged for me to attend. I do not know who paid my tuition, but my hunch is that Ma Baker had a hand in it.

THE PALMER MEMORIAL INSTITUTE was an all-black coeducational high school in Sedalia, North Carolina, which is near Greensboro, where the sit-in movement began. Palmer Memorial, I was to learn, was founded in 1902 by Charlotte Hawkins, a pioneer in education for African Americans. Despite great travails, Hawkins turned a one-room building into a thriving campus and a leader in the education of black youth in North Carolina.

Before I started school at Palmer, Mrs. Baker took me to New York City—for the second time in one year, which was especially remarkable considering I had scarcely ever been outside Mississippi before I turned seventeen. Mrs. Baker had an apartment in New York. She took me around the city and bought me a suitcase for my trip to Palmer Memorial. She even taught me how to pack a suitcase to maximize what you could stuff into it. She had traveled so much in the 1940s–1960s that she knew all the tricks. She showed me that if I rolled my clothing instead of folding it, I could get far more into a suitcase.

In September 1962, I began my sophomore year of high school at Palmer Memorial. My fellow students came from all over, but I was the only one from Mississippi and the only one who had been involved in civil rights activities. Many of my fellow students came from affluent black families and could not relate to a civil rights activist who came from a poor Mississippi family. While I made friends with some of the girls at the school, the atmosphere was rigid and conservative. When I mentioned my involvement with civil rights and what that had led to, I found that the other students were not really receptive, so I stopped talking about it.

I was still suffering at that time, and the atmosphere at Palmer was not helpful. The school ran by the clock. We students lived in dorms and lights came on and went off at a certain time. Classes ran Monday through Friday. On some weekends, we could travel to Greensboro, but that was our only respite from the school regimen. Palmer reminded me in many ways of Oakley. It was like being in a prison, which was not a prison. All of our actions and activities were planned and monitored and everything had to be done together and timely. I found the atmosphere as suffocating as Oakley had been. My sense of being alone was more acute at Palmer than at any time in my life before or since. While I was in an all-black school, much as I had been while growing up in Mc-Comb, I had no one to confide in, to bare my heart and soul. I was still experiencing flashbacks and nightmares from my experience with the Fischers. I could not let myself cry, as I feared that if I let myself go, I would never recover. I was truly a lost soul. I felt as if the walls were closing in.

IN THE FALL OF 1962, an event occurred which would set me on another road, at least for the following year. I received a letter from a doctor and her family who lived in the Chicago area. Dr. Vera Markovin King wrote and invited me to come to Chicago for the Christmas holidays of 1962. As strange as it may seem, the letter I received from Dr. Markovin King was not unusual. Since my story had been published in *Jet* and in SNCC newsletters, I would often receive letters, both while I was in Atlanta and at Palmer, offering a home for me to visit or for a vacation. While I was touched then and am still touched today by the outpouring of generosity towards me by many people who only knew me from my story, I was at the time suffering from an acute "trust" problem. After what I had experienced with my last "savior," how was I to trust that these too-good-to-be-true people were actually sincere and would not try to hurt me. But for reasons that I cannot recall now, I decided to go to Chicago for the Christmas holidays—I could not go home to Mississippi, as I was banned, and I could not stay alone at Palmer for the holidays.

Dr. Markovin King and her husband, Leo King, were the first interracial couple I had known. Indeed, in 1962, interracial marriage was illegal in many states, including my home state. The Kings lived in Maywood, a Chicago suburb, with their three children, who were high school students like me. They treated me warmly while I was with them for the holidays and I enjoyed my time with them, even my first experience with snow. Before I went back to North Carolina, Dr. King told me that I was always welcome at the Kings' home and that her family would like for me to come to Chicago when I finished my school year at Palmer and live with them and their children. I made no commitment at the time, but the offer was intriguing. I was truly unhappy at Palmer, and there was something in me that would continue to persist for some time that I needed to move on, that staying in one place for too long was somehow dangerous, stifling. I was restless and an offer to go elsewhere was welcomed.

I returned to Palmer at the end of my vacation. I resolved to focus my energies on my studies, and I did well, if not exceptionally. My thoughts would often drift back to my time in Chicago. Here was a family that genuinely wanted me to be part of them, and I longed for a family since I had been uprooted from my own.

I made up my mind to accept the Kings' offer to move to Chicago, but there was one large hurdle. How was I going to tell Ella Baker of my decision? I owed so much to her and I knew that someone, perhaps Mrs. Baker herself, had sacrificed a great deal for me to attend Palmer. I did not want to seem ungrateful, but I knew that I had to escape my latest prison and the Kings' offer was my escape mechanism. However, I misjudged Ma Baker. As she did with all of us who she nurtured, and she nurtured many, she listened intently to me. She believed in youth and believed in youth making our own decisions. I was relieved, and when the school year ended, I was off on a new nomadic venture, this time to Chicago.

Before actually moving to Chicago, I was to spend the summer at a camp that Dr. Markovin King operated in Dalton, Michigan, near Kalamazoo. The camp was called the Circle Pines Center, and she and her family, including her sons, would attend for the entire summer. It was understood that I was attending on a scholarship or grant and I would need to work to help defray my expenses. I spent my working hours at the nursery and spent the remainder of my time involved in camp activities. I enjoyed the summer and the change from the very staid atmosphere at Palmer.

When the summer was over, I went with the King family to their home in Maywood, Illinois. I started my junior year at Proviso East High School. Proviso East was an integrated school, fairly evenly balanced between white and black students.* Again, academically I did fine, but the same lingering doubts kept me from interacting freely with the other students, particularly the white students. While this was the first time I had attended school with whites, I tended to stick with King family members and other black students.

---

* One of my fellow students, though I did not know him at the time, was Fred Hampton, who like me began his civil rights involvement with an NAACP youth chapter. Later he would lead the Black Panther Party in Chicago and be assassinated by the Chicago police/FBI in 1969.

As I had issues with the social aspects at school, I also began to experience difficulties with the Kings, most particularly Dr. King. As I look back over many years at my experiences, I recognize that the Kings were well-intentioned, and I was the person having difficulty relating to them. Something inside of me was always in turmoil. It was more than just the normal upheaval of the teenage years. I liked Mr. King and could more readily relate to him, as he was a Southerner, having come originally from Arkansas. I was the only one in the family who could call Leo "Pops" and get away with it. I also related well to the Kings' sons and communicate with them today. But whenever I would get too close, whatever was inside me would pull me back. I could not allow myself to become too comfortable because I was always expecting something bad to happen.

Before long, I felt the need to move on again, and that opportunity soon came my way. However, before I moved on, I stayed with the Kings for the summer of 1963.

During that summer, I experienced the same viciousness of racism in the North as I had experienced in the South. The Kings had sold their home in Maywood and bought a home in another area of Chicago, the virtually all-white suburb of Oak Park. The interracial Kings were not welcomed there with open arms, to put it mildly. They had bought their house through a white straw buyer, much as the white civil rights activists Carl and Anne Braden had done for a black family in a celebrated earlier case in Louisville, Kentucky. In Oak Park, when the Kings and I actually moved into the new home and the "good" people of the neighborhood realized who we were, the harassment began. Our home was pelted with eggs and there were other hostile gestures that made it clear that we were not wanted in Oak Park. While I had experienced hostility in the South before, that hostility was mostly related to my civil rights activity. The hostility that I experienced that summer in the North was new to me, and let me see that the struggle I had participated in in the South was national in scope and far greater than I had ever imagined. At the end of summer, I was ready to continue my wandering ways.

I HAD RECEIVED ANOTHER offer to take me in from a Connecticut family headed by a professor at Yale Law School. Although I did not know it at the time, Mr. Thomas Emerson was a very involved and committed person. Shortly after graduating from Yale Law School in 1931, Mr. Emerson became one of the lawyers involved with the Scottsboro Boys, the nine young black men who were sentenced to death in Alabama for allegedly raping two white women. Later, Mr. Emerson worked in the Franklin Roosevelt administration helping craft New Deal legislation. Two years after the Emersons first contacted me, Mr. Emerson argued a case in the United States Supreme Court that ended Connecticut's ban on the sale of contraceptives.

However, it was not Mr. Emerson who reached out to me, but rather it was Ruth Emerson, his second wife. She had been a school teacher, but had retired to be a homemaker and help raise the three Emerson children, their mother having died. Mrs. Emerson was an exceedingly warm person, as I believe were all of the other people—except the Fischers—with whom I stayed. But I had such difficulty accepting that warmth.

However, I did accept the Emersons' offer to come live with them and spend my senior year of high school in North Haven, Connecticut.

My experiences in Connecticut began the extremely slow process of restoring trust in my life. The Emersons, particularly Mrs. Emerson, treated me truly as a daughter. Their three children, two sons and a daughter, were equally welcoming. The city that we lived in, North Haven, was unlike anything I had experienced before. North Haven is an upscale community, virtually all white—North

Haven High School had only two black students, me and a young man. While I felt the warmth at home, I did not always feel that I fit in this upscale white world. I was the product of an extremely poverty-stricken community in Mississippi juxtaposed with children of privilege who never knew what it was like to miss a meal, who had all the material things anyone could want, including educational opportunities that far exceeded anything that I could ever imagine. While I was clearly out of my element, an inner strength, even if I doubted at times, plus the promise I had made to my mother that I would finish high school, kept me going.

I was introduced to many new things in Connecticut. One vivid memory is of my fellow students at North Haven High School being convinced that they were going to teach this product of the South how to roller skate. There were no roller rinks in McComb, and if there had been, they would have been for whites only. But one evening we all trooped to the roller rink. After getting the skates on my feet, my classmates led me around the rink, with a student balancing me at each side. We must have been quite a sight, this group of white students leading the only black student by the hand around the rink. When they decided that I had learned enough and could manage on my own, they let go of me. I protested that I was not ready, but all in vain. Suddenly, my legs went out from under me and I went flying in the air and crashed down on my behind so hard that if my butt had been glass, it would have shattered all over the rink. My fellow students, in tears from laughing so hard, helped me up and got me off the rink. I have never been in a roller rink since.

Some of my rebellious spirit remained, but for the most part it was kept in check in Connecticut. However, there was one incident in which I let this restless spirit take over. The Emersons' home was right across the street from the home of the chief of police. In his yard, the chief had one of those decorative mock hitching posts fashioned as a statue of a black-faced jockey. These were once fairly common in white people's yards. Seeing that racist symbol every day ate at me until I knew I had to do something. I raised the issue with the Emersons' youngest son, Lee, then a student at Yale, who shared some of my rebellious spirit. The two of us conspired, and late one evening we grabbed some white paint and paint brushes and went across the street and gave the jockey a white face. The next morning when people saw what had happened, everyone wondered who did it. Lee and I just smiled inwardly and never told anyone that we were responsible.

The school year went fast, and in June 1964, a year after I should have graduated, I received a diploma from North Haven High School. I was proud of this accomplishment as it had come despite great obstacles. Over a four-year period, I had attended four very different high schools, in four states, under extreme circumstances.

But I had graduated (as did all of my siblings), and I had lived up to the promise that I made to my mother.

Sources of Photographs

Page 87: top, courtesy of John Hardy; middle, *Jet* magazine; bottom, courtesy of Matt Williamson, *McComb Enterprise-Journal*.

Page 88: top, courtesy of AP; inset, courtesy of Charla Johns; bottom, courtesy of Paul Richards/ Harvey Richards Media Archive.

Page 89: courtesy of Matt Williamson, *McComb Enterprise-Journal*.

Page 90: top and middle, courtesy of Matt Williamson, *McComb Enterprise-Journal*. Bottom, courtesy of Charla Johns.

Page 91: top and middle, courtesy of Matt Williamson, *McComb Enterprise-Journal*.

Except as indicated above, all photos were provided by Brenda Travis.

Left: I was 16 when I began working with the NAACP on voter registration in my hometown of McComb, Mississippi.
Below: With my mother, in the few moments we had together before my 1962 exile from Mississippi.

Left: SNCC workers Marion Barry and James Bevel with high school walkout student Johnye Wilcher in McComb, 1961.

Above: the walkout at Burglund High School, 1962. Right: The Illinois Central Railroad viaduct separates white McComb from black McComb; this was along the walkout students' route to city hall. Below: the movement arrives in McComb— Bob Moses, Hollis Watkins, and Curtis Hayes, 1961.

Top left: Aylene Quin is second from left at a meeting in 1960s. Top right: A SNCC rally with Bob Moses in foreground. Inset: a 1961 protest march over Mississippi's voting laws. Above: Bob Zellner, right, with fellow SNCC activist Cliff Vaughs, 1961.

Top: C. C. Bryant's barbershop after bombing. Middle: March on Pike County Courthouse. Bottom: The Masonic Temple today; its upper level was used as SNCC headquarters, where organizing, rallies and voter education classes took place.

Above:
Society Hill
Missionary
Baptist Church
in McComb
was bombed
on the night of
September 20,
1964. Below:
Mrs. Alyene
Quin's home
was bombed
the same
night; two
children and a
babysitter were
in the home at
the time.

Receiving
the Louis M.
Weintraub
Award in
New York
City, 1962.

Top: Speaking in McComb at the William Winter Reconciliation Conference, 2006. Inset: We had a commemorative cake at the October 2016 anniversary of the Burglund Walkout. Bottom left: The first black mayor of McComb, Zachery Patterson, welcomed guests at the 55th anniversary celebration. Bottom right: Civil rights icon Bob Moses also spoke.

Above: Present-day City of McComb selectmen Ronnie Brock and Donovan Hill flank Bob Moses after he was presented a Key to the City. Right: They presented a Key to me at the same time. Below: Later, City Councilman Joe Lewis (back row, far right) presented similar Keys to us from the City of Summit. Bob and I were joined by a dozen other veterans of the 1960s' civil rights struggle in McComb and surrounding areas.

Right: Fifty years after being exiled, I was overcome with emotion when presented with an honorary diploma after fifty years.

Center: Youth from the McComb Oral History Project interviewing me at Urban School of San Francisco, California.

Bottom: In San Francisco with Lyderious Isaac, DeLisa Magee, LaToya Smith, Vickie Malone, and Alexander Fletcher.

At the Veterans of the Mississippi Civil Rights Movement conference: top, with John Hardy; middle, with Afena Shakur, Tupac's mother; bottom, with James Kates, a Freedom Summer volunteer.

From left, three courageous women of strength, me, Euvester Simpson, and Frankye Adams Johnson

More reunions at the Veterans of the Mississippi Civil Rights Movement conference

Above, with Alice Walker

Right, with Jimmie Travis, who was wounded near Greenwood, and later was the founding chair of the VMCRM; bottom, my great-nephew, Christian James Webb, with Owen Brooks's daughter, Pam.

Right: at the William Winter Reconciliation Conference, 2006, with Randall O'Brien and my brother James; holding the Bronze Star that Randall presented to me.

Below, with Randall at Carson-Newman University in Jefferson City, Tennessee.

11

The Lure of Mississippi

My Connecticut "family" wanted me to stay on with them after I graduated from high school, but in my heart I knew that I needed to go home to Mississippi. During the school year, I had contemplated what I would do next. I knew it would have something to do with Mississippi.

Though I had been banned by then-Governor Barnett, the risk of going back to Mississippi did not frighten me. I knew I had to take this enemy head-on, as I have always done. I had remained in contact with many friends in my other family, the SNCC people, and they had told me about their plans for the summer of 1964. A large contingent of students from the North, mostly white, were being recruited to come to Mississippi to do what we had done in 1961 in McComb, to register voters. The concept, which came to be called Freedom Summer, was to open the eyes of the country to conditions in my state. The hope was that this would bring enough pressure to end the reign of tyranny over my people.

While I was not recruited as a volunteer, I was invited to attend the training sessions in Oxford, Ohio, for those who were going to Mississippi. I have read over the years about the Highlander School in Tennessee where blacks and whites were brought together in the 1950s to find solutions to segregation in the South, as well as in the North. My experience in Ohio and the experience for many of the students must have been comparable to what Rosa Parks experienced at Highlander—a community of like-minded people, black and white, working together harmoniously to find solutions to the race issue in our country.

I sat in on many of the training sessions. I was introduced by my SNCC brothers and sisters as one who had bravely taken a stand and had valiantly suffered the consequences. Many of the white students were my age and had never interacted with a black person before, but they listened intently to my story and those of other veterans of the Mississippi wars. While I had met a number of SNCC workers in McComb in 1961, I now met a number of new faces who became involved after 1961. One was Willie Peacock, later known as Wazir, who became a friend for life and was instrumental later in my nomadic ventures.

A pivotal event in Ohio stands out in my memory. I recall the session that all of us were in when Bob Moses addressed the group. Bob, whom I had admired from my first involvement with him in McComb, started speaking to the group slowly and haltingly. With a painful expression on his face, he announced to the group that three of the volunteers—one on his first day in Mississippi—had gone missing. Many writers have described the scene in Ohio on that day, but my memory is that there was a collective, audible gasp from the attendees, with cries of "Oh, no." We who were from Mississippi knew instantly and instinctively that "missing" meant "dead," as that was the pattern in Mississippi. But the difference here was that two of the missing young men were white. While the Reverend George Lee, Herbert Lee, and Medgar Evers had been killed for their involvement in civil rights, no whites had up to now suffered such consequences.

The discussions after Bob's announcement were intense. A lot of tears were shed that day. Most who had volunteered understood intellectually that there was a risk of being hurt. Suddenly that risk became very real. Death is not something that registers with nineteen- or twenty-year-olds, but death was a real possibility for those who were venturing into Mississippi for the first time. These students learned what we black native Mississippians always knew, that there was a great danger in seeking progress for black people. I learned afterwards that despite the harsh dose of reality, none of the students chose to go home.

UNLIKE THE NORTHERN STUDENTS who received specific assignments after their training at Oxford, I did not have a specific project that I would work on. I knew that there would be a project for me somewhere, as there always had been, but the first item on my agenda after Oxford was to go home. I knew there was going to be a big push in McComb with SNCC veterans and newly arrived Northern students, the first such big push for civil rights since the events of 1961, when the movement pulled out of McComb because it was too dangerous at the time. For me, I just wanted to go home, to see my family for the first time in years and be back in the warmth of my mother, who was again living in McComb.

How did I dare return to Mississippi, when I was banned from the state, a ban that has never been lifted, even as of today? I just did! For reasons that I will never be able to explain, I never believed that Mississippi government officials would actually enforce the ban against me. Despite a risk of being jailed, I needed to return to my home, which is and will likely always be, Mississippi.

The reunion with my family was joyous, with hugs, kisses and some tears. While she would never tell me this, when I looked in my mother's eyes for the first time in two years, I could see the strain. She had not been beaten down, but the years had taken a toll on my beloved mother. And while I did not feel guilt over my part in her pain, I did feel responsible and knew that in time I would have to give back to my mother for all she had given me.

While I spent a good part of the summer of 1964 in Jackson,

where my brother was a student at Jackson State University, I was actively aware of what was going on in McComb. McComb in the summer of 1964 can only be described as a terrorist's paradise. Members of the Association for the Preservation of the White Race vied with the Klan for which group could inflict the most harm on activist community members. If Birmingham, Alabama, was often referred to as Bombingham, there should be a similar name for McComb as there were more bombings in McComb than in any comparable city. C. C. Bryant's home and barber shop were bombed. Aylene Quin's home was bombed while her children, Jacqueline and Anthony, were in the home with a babysitter and were injured. What was the police response? To take into custody the babysitter and the friend who was with her. On the same day the Quin home was bombed, one of the churches whose members were active in the movement, Society Hill Missionary Baptist Church, was bombed. We can only be thankful that there was no loss of life at Society Hill, but the devastation to the church was total.

While I was hearing about these horror stories in McComb and could see the devastation firsthand when I would make visits to my home, I spent my time in Jackson involved in projects with SNCC workers and members of the Mississippi Freedom Democratic Party (MFDP).* In Jackson, I stayed at the home of Lawrence Guyot, who was to head the MFDP. I worked with Guyot—everyone simply called him "Guyot"—on many of the MFDP activities, and through that involvement I was privileged to meet other women activists, including Fannie Lou Hamer, Victoria Gray Adams, and Annie Devine. These women, much as Ella Baker before them, inspired my own activism, knowing that there was a role for me to play in bringing about change. In that summer of 1964, I worked hand in hand with Guyot to, among other things, oppose pending

---

* Formed as an alternative to the segregated regular state Democratic Party.

legislation in the Mississippi House of Representatives that would have mandated sterilization for black women with two or more children. Genocide by another name!

In August 1964, I went to Atlantic City with the MFDP delegation to the Democratic National Convention. The buses that took us to Atlantic City were filled with hopeful black people who were for the first time participating in our democratic process, such as it proved to be.

I attended many of the convention events and witnessed on the boardwalk the drawings of the three young civil rights workers whose bodies had recently been found and the hulk of the burned-out car that they were last seen in. I shared the hopes of the MFDP delegates and mourned with them when a president scuttled their challenge because he was more interested in insuring his election than standing for the moral principle on which the challenge was based. I could also see the toll that the defeat took on Bob Moses and other of my SNCC activist friends, who had such high hopes that were shattered in the face of blind ambition. While I shared their pain, I realized that the challenges we faced were of an ongoing nature and we simply had to continue the struggle.

Through Guyot, I became director of an adult education program in Meridian, Mississippi. The Freedom Schools established by SNCC across Mississippi in 1964 had demonstrated the serious need to improve the state's educational system. They also, along with the voter registration drive, brought to light the serious issue of illiteracy among Mississippi's adult African Americans. These men and women were being asked to register to vote when many of them could not sign their own names, let alone read the complicated forms that Mississippi required to be able to register. It was no wonder they could not read, because for many years, especially in the rural areas, education for blacks was simply not available. My own father was a victim of this discrimination.

In Meridian, we set up a program to address adult illiteracy and reached out to black teachers to spend their evening hours working with these education-starved adults. At first we met resistance from many of the teachers, but when they experienced firsthand the rewards of seeing an adult for the first time reading a sentence, or writing his or her name, they became enthusiastic supporters.

IN THE FALL OF 1965, a new opportunity opened for me. I had remained in contact with my Illinois and Connecticut families, and Dr. Markovin King reached out to me. A young minister, Jesse Jackson, who was involved with Dr. Martin Luther King Jr. in the Southern Christian Leadership Conference, was starting a new program to address the serious problem of urban poverty in the North. The project was called Operation Breadbasket, and because it was only in its infancy, there were no offices; Reverend Jackson was working out of his home. I welcomed the opportunity to be at the ground level of a new activist organization and accepted a position with Operation Breadbasket. I essentially performed all secretarial and clerical functions for the new operation.

The summer of 1966 brought another change. I made my first trip that year to California, the state that would become my home for almost the next fifty years. The reason for the move was love, or at least that's what I thought. I had met a young man in Mississippi. I liked him a lot and he lured me to California. I did not know that he was married and had a pregnant wife, although he was not living with her. Soon after I came to California, he was gone. I needed to make decisions as to the course my life would take. Many of the SNCC activists were no longer working in the South, and I reached out to one of them who was then in Los Angeles.

Wazir Peacock, whom I had met in Ohio, was working with the Greater Los Angeles Community Action program. He welcomed a call from a fellow activist, explained what GLACA did, and invited me to join the organization as a community organizer. GLACA organizers would go out into the poor black and Latino communities of Los Angeles and organize meetings with community leaders and residents. At these meetings, we would reach out to impoverished members of the community to advise them as to resources that they might not be aware of, for example, where and how to get help with paying utility bills, where and how to get help in dealing with unscrupulous landlords, and, my favorite and old standby, how to go about registering to vote.

Because working with GLACA gave me a lot of freedom to practice what I had learned from my earliest days of civil rights involvement in Mississippi, I enjoyed the work very much. I was also free to take unpaid time off to pursue other opportunities, one of which led me back to Mississippi for a period of time while on sabbatical from GLACA. The ACLU had set up a program in Jackson headed by the well-known civil rights lawyer, Armand Derfner. To get the program off the ground, they needed a typist/receptionist, and I filled that role. Being back in Mississippi, even for a short period of time, let me keep a closer eye on my mother, as I continued to be concerned with her health.

After a brief time working with the ACLU program in Mississippi, I returned to Los Angeles and GLACA.

By the late 1960s, it became clear to me that programs such as GLACA, which were part of the Great Society* anti-poverty programs, were not going to survive. Like many of my fellow activists, I was faced with a new challenge. I had neglected my education to pursue activism. I had learned many skills along the way, but in translating those skills into job opportunities, I was constantly faced with the "great skills/no degree" dilemma. As a result, I did two things. First, I obtained a job with an insurance company in its

---

* President Lyndon Johnson's umbrella of social service anti-poverty programs.

steno pool and moved from there to become the executive secretary for the director of an HMO. Second, I went back to school, ultimately taking business-related classes at a school in Burbank from which I obtained a certificate of completion. I knew that I would need additional education if I was to have long-term opportunities, and I enrolled in a program and took night classes while I worked during the day.

IN THE 1970S, I married for the first and only time. He was from Louisiana. He was divorced and had two boys, fourteen and twelve. I think he was expecting me to raise the children. I liked the boys, but soon grew to dislike my husband because he was a womanizer. The marriage was a disaster and did not last long. I take full responsibility for its failure. However, being married, even for a short time, rekindled trust issues that I thought I had resolved after my jailing, reform school, and my experience with Professor Fischer. In a one-on-one relationship, the issues that I had with trusting any husband proved deadly.

In 1973, I took a new job in California's university system, specifically at Cal State Northridge. There is always a delightful recognition of irony for those of us who have been involved in the civil rights movement to later obtain jobs at institutions that, but for the civil rights movement, would never have admitted us or hired us. I had heard that Cal State Northridge was slow to admit black students, let alone African American professors or staff. Indeed, the position that I obtained was as secretary in the black studies department, a relatively new department. Early on, I learned the ways of both the department and the university and the treatment of its workers, which led me to become active in the university employees' union and also to become a union steward.

One event from my employment at the university stands out in my memory and takes me back to my civil rights days. Cal State

Northridge, as did other universities at this time, had a very active student body. In the days when the United States' divestiture of its assets in South Africa was a civil rights issue, the students became active and vocal and even occupied university buildings in protest of apartheid. Because I had experienced apartheid in our own country, I applauded the students' actions and joined them in the takeover of the administration building, sleeping with them overnight in the building. I was the only staff person to risk my status with the university to sit-in with the students, but because I had encountered far worse in Mississippi, I did not think the risk was too great.

While I was working at Cal State, two pivotal events took place that would alter my life plan. The first involved my mother. I was traveling to Mississippi as often as I could to see my mom and my family. On my visits, I could see my mother's health declining. Medical care in Mississippi, particularly for African Americans, was poor at best, and for an African American woman of extremely limited means, good health care was nonexistent. In my phone conversations over the years with my mom, I encouraged her to join me in California, so I could help her obtain quality medical care. As might be expected, she was resistant, suggesting that I was just trying to lure her out to California to live with me. She did not want to leave Mississippi, nor did she want to become a burden on me, as she knew that my position at the university was stressful.

After many coaxing conversations, I finally persuaded her to come to California, but strings were attached. She agreed to come for two weeks if I bought her a round-trip ticket, which I did. She never used the return portion of the ticket, but rather stayed in California obtaining much-needed medical care. Once she decided to stay in California, it was clear that she would not be able to work, though she tried for a while, and that she would need a lot of care, in addition to the medical intervention. I made a decision at this point in my life to be my mom's primary caregiver.

The decision was relatively easy, although it meant giving up something important to me—my education. I had continued to pursue my education while employed at Cal State Northridge, but to give my mom the care she needed, I had to give up my hopes for the degree I coveted. While I have always felt a loss in not having a degree, my decision to become my mom's primary caregiver came not only from my family roots but also out of a sense of responsibility. I knew that my going to jail, to the reformatory, and being exiled from Mississippi had affected my mother emotionally, psychologically, and even physically. She, like many others who had children active in the movement, paid as great a price as I had, as she lost her ability to care for herself and my siblings. That toll not only affected her but many other black families in Mississippi and elsewhere in the South. Taking care of her was my way of giving back to her and assuming responsibility for my actions. It was a heavy burden, but a welcome one.

The months and years that I was my mom's caretaker were special for me. As happens in many families, there was a role reversal, with the child, now an adult, being the primary caregiver. But in my case, it was even more special. While my mother had been and would always be the most important individual in my life, here was an opportunity to quietly and sometimes not so quietly interact one-on-one and get to better know the one great love of my life. As my mother struggled with her health-related issues, I could only revel in her great strength in the face of adversity. We would talk of many things, of her hard life growing up, of the importance of family, and of her admiration for my taking a stand for civil rights, but also of my admiration for how she had toughed it out because of my activities. The time that I spent with my mom was healing;

it restored much of the trust that had been missing in my life. As I write these words, tears form, as I miss my mom greatly, but I credit this very strong woman with making me whole again.

The second pivotal event that took place in my life involved my dad. I began a search for my dad. Or, differently put, I began a search for something that I felt was missing in myself—something that caused me to focus on the father I never knew.

Why was it that my relationships with men were short-lived and, like my marriage, ended in disaster? What in me was lacking? Why was it that I could not trust? These questions led me to believe that some answers might be found in a search for the missing link in my life, my dad. But how does one go about finding someone who disappeared many years ago and about whom I knew little beyond his name because over the years, my mother had said very little about my dad, nothing good, and nothing bad. Nothing. How do you find someone who could not be found even by the white folks who hunted him?

I began to do some research, trying for the most part to keep my mother out of this quest, as I was not sure how it would impact her. I managed to find some scraps of information. Before my mom and dad married, my dad had previously been married and had two children by that marriage, a boy and a girl. I found out the name of the boy, who like my dad, only had initials: "L. C." But then I found out the tragedy of my half-brother's life. He, like so many of our young, black men of today, wound up in the prison system and was in one of the worst hellholes in the United States, Angola Prison, in Louisiana. I reached out to him by letter, which felt strange, as he knew nothing of me or my dad's second family. Amazingly enough, he was receptive to me, but he had no idea of our dad's whereabouts. He did still have contact with his sister, who was equally without information about our father but put me in touch with his surviving sibling, Wilhemena, who lived in Chicago. Much to my surprise when I contacted this aunt, whom I also never knew, she not only knew where my dad lived, Louisiana, but she had a phone number where he could be reached.

How does one make a phone call to someone you don't know but who has been constantly in the dark, murky background of your being. I imagined myself as an adopted child who with great difficulty had tracked down her birth parents. What kind of reception would I receive? A hang-up? Rejection? Warmth and love was too much to be expected for two virtual strangers, but perhaps just some explanations of a life about which I knew nothing. I got so much more.

With some trepidation, I placed the phone call to my dad. In my imagination, I had expected the deep baritone voice of a strong man, but I received a typical Southern black man's voice, somewhat high-pitched. I got straight to the point and told him that I was his daughter, Brenda, that I had searched long and hard for him because I wanted to find my dad.

I was stunned when he immediately broke down and cried, a totally unexpected response. I began to tear up myself, as we made small talk—where I lived, what I did, did I have children, how was my mother and where was she? He explained that some years before he had returned to McComb only to find that his wife no longer lived there, nor many of my siblings.

In that initial conversation, we did not go into depth about the where's and how's of my dad's life. That would have to wait. I had many, many questions, but I resisted the urge to press this man, whom I knew not at all, to reveal information that I suspected would be painful for him to tell and, I suspected, painful for me to hear. I did tell him that Mom was living with me in California. With the same headstrong manner which has served me well in life, in that very first conversation with my dad, I invited him to come to California to visit me, my mom, and my sisters who were living in California.

As my mother initially had, my dad protested that he could not come to California. His roots were now in Louisiana, he had never been on a plane, and on and on. It was remarkable how similar his response was to that of my mom when I had first invited her to come. But after several more phone conversations, I persuaded him, bought him a ticket, and he was on his way.

Mom, my sister Marionette, and I went to Los Angeles airport in May 1981 to await my dad's arrival. When he got off the plane, we were there to greet him, two of his grown children, and my mom. When he spotted us, or more correctly spotted my mom, as he would not have recognized me or Marionette without my mom, my dad again broke down and cried. This was another response I had not expected, as the men I knew did not cry, perceiving it as unmanly. As we all hugged each other and cried, my dad did another thing that was totally unexpected. He first asked my mother for forgiveness, and then he asked me and my sister for forgiveness. We all told him that there was nothing to ask forgiveness for, as we were now together, and together we would begin a new chapter in our lives.

LIKE MY MOTHER BEFORE him, my dad never went back to Louisiana; Mom and I persuaded him to stay in California. With my mom and dad now both living in California with me, I assumed the parenting role for both of them, a parenting role that I was never fortunate to have with children of my own. Over the next months and years, slowly and sometimes tearfully, I learned the story of my dad's life, of early days without parents of his own, of his marriage to my mom, of their moving to the Delta, and of his having to flee for his life.

If I thought my life was one of exile, I realized that my dad's was far more difficult than mine. I had the good fortune of being taken in by families—except for Professor Fischer—who loved, cared for, and nurtured me while I was in exile. But my dad had none of these family amenities. His life was the life of many black men on the move, taking jobs where they could be found, working in the fields as a day laborer, or working in the lumber mills. His stay in one place could not last long, as he was always looking over his shoulder, afraid that if he became too close to anyone, information about his past might come out and he would be on the run again. He was like "The Fugitive" of the 1960s television show, without any of the glamor, but with a need to be constantly on the move, not from a one-armed man and the law but from the white man's law in Mississippi.

Over the months that my dad and mom lived with me, a respect and then a love grew. We became a family together, sharing the love, quibbling, and good and bad times that are part of all families.

In the late-1980s, after I was forced to retire from the university system because of my own severe health issues, I could no longer care for my mom and dad in the way that I wanted to, because of their deteriorating health. I did find a senior assisted-care facility near me where both of them could live, though unfortunately not as husband and wife because if they had so identified themselves, they could not have afforded the facility. Then in 1998, eight months apart, my parents died. Right before my dad died, he said some words that will always be with me. He said, "Baby, while you never had any of your own children, you were a mother to many," including him, my dad. When I think about the horrible life he had, those words are of great comfort to me, as I was able to give him something he never had before—love, mothering, and a family.

While my dad's death, although expected, shook me, there are hardly words that can describe the loss I felt when my mom died. As my mother's health deteriorated, I was filled with dread. She was always the one constant in my life, no matter how far away from each other we were. She was a brave, strong woman, which I aspired to be. As she slowly slipped away from me, I began to feel inconsolable sorrow. My sisters, Marionette and Gloria, tried mightily to support me during those final hours, I felt more alone than I had ever been, even more alone than at Oakley or Palmer Institute. When mom died, quietly and peacefully, a certain peace came over me. While tears flowed, I knew that somehow, some way, I would carry on, as I was her legacy, and I was now the standard-bearer for the family, who would now look to me for the same nurturing and strength that we had always looked to from mom. I have tried to carry on this legacy for my mom, if imperfectly.

When my dad died, I respected his wishes, and he was cremated and buried in California. He had no desire to return to Mississippi, even in death. My mother, on the other hand, never got Mississippi out of her heart and soul and wanted to be buried in the state of her birth. We flew my mom's body back to Mississippi and buried her in McComb. While I have not made a final decision, I believe that I would like to be buried in Mississippi, near my mother, so I can never be exiled from Mississippi again.

12

McComb and Change

Since 1961 and 1962, when I took my stand and was exiled from Mississippi and McComb, I have traveled back to the community of my birth on many occasions. In the fifty-plus years that have gone by, I have witnessed real change in my hometown, but I have also witnessed events that purported to reflect positive change but in fact were more of what I had encountered in my youth. Lastly, I have witnessed change for the worse, which has caused me to redirect my energies in my later years to continue what I began in 1961—to bring fairness and justice to all of the citizens of my community. While my methods may be somewhat different today, my commitment has never wavered.

When I look at McComb today, I see many superficial changes in the community. In 1961, the streets in Baertown and the two other black sections of McComb were dirt or gravel; today they are paved. Indeed, some of these paved streets have new names. With the 2006 election of Zachary Patterson, the first African American mayor in McComb's history, four streets in McComb were renamed for local African American heroes. Three of the four streets honor my mentor, C. C. Bryant; L. J. Martin, the first black man to run for elective office in McComb; and Frank Mingo, who ironically is the person responsible for the streets being paved in the black community. The fourth street and the only one named for an

African American woman is Brenda Travis Street, which fittingly is one block over from C. C. Bryant Street. I did not, nor have I ever, sought recognition such as this, but unbeknownst to me, some of my family members who continue to live in McComb thought it only appropriate that the street where we grew up be renamed for a local heroine, who risked all to effect change, even though the change I sought to make had nothing to do with street signs.

There has been additional positive, superficial change. In my youth there were no street lights in Baertown, but today there are some. Whereas my brothers and sisters had to go to our neighbors' houses to pump water from their wells, today most of the homes in the black community have running water. Where my brothers and sisters had to go outdoors in the cold winter or hot summer days to use the outhouse, those outhouses—which were often tipped over by Halloween pranksters—have disappeared, replaced by the sanitary sewers that white McComb always had. Restaurants and theaters—to the extent that any theaters exist in McComb proper—and stores of every kind are frequented equally by blacks and whites, and blacks are employed in many of these facilities. But if one looks beyond these outward changes, one sees that much has not changed. Two such instances, both of which I was directly involved with, demonstrate that the steps we made forward were followed by steps backward.

WHILE I WOULD RETURN to McComb on a regular basis, I spent my time with family and friends and was not directly involved in the affairs of the community. Thus, I was not aware that in 2004 the mayor of McComb had invited the William Winter Institute for Racial Reconciliation at the University of Mississippi to come to McComb to help improve race relations in the city. The Winter Institute was established in the late 1990s by former Governor Winter to be a catalyst for improving race relations throughout the state by establishing forums on race-related issues. This included the promotion of the teaching of the history of the civil rights movement in the public schools.

Over the next two years, through the efforts chiefly of Susan Glisson, director of the Institute, programs were initiated in McComb through the municipal offices and through the school board and school superintendent to address issues within the community. Dr. Pat Cooper, then the school superintendent, appeared to be an enthusiastic supporter of Ms. Glisson's proposals to incorporate the teaching of civil rights in the McComb public schools. But as I was to later learn, Dr. Cooper had a hidden agenda. While heartily endorsing the Winter Institute's programs, he was at the same time trying to undermine racial progress. McComb's schools were finally fully integrated the 1970s under a "consent decree" issued by a federal court as a result of a lawsuit under the principles established by *Brown v. Board of Education* two decades earlier. Dr. Cooper, it turned out, was taking steps to have the consent decree lifted. Most of McComb's black educators viewed this as his attempt to totally control the school district at the cost of equality in the school system.

In 2005, the Winter Institute, in conjunction with the city and the school board, conducted a workshop at the McComb High School in observance of Martin Luther King Jr. Day. One of the coordinators of the event on behalf of the city was a classmate from my school days, Jackie Martin Byrd, who had walked out with me and the others when I was expelled in 1961. I did not attend the conference, but Bob Moses came back to McComb for the first time since the 1960s to participate in it. In addition, Curtis Hayes (now Curtis Hayes Muhammad), who along with Hollis Watkins was the first to take direct action to integrate facilities in McComb and who had inspired me to step forward, was the keynote speaker at the event. Curtis told the audience of the many sacrifices that he and others, including me, had made to bring about change in McComb, but he also pointed out that for the most part our actions had been forgotten as history had moved on. The event inspired additional programs within the community.

One of those programs was to involve me in a way which reminded me how little real progress has been made in race relations within my city. As Ms. Glisson, whom I often affectionately refer to as my "sister," related, some members of the McComb school board staff approached her. Plans were being laid to hold in McComb a second statewide civil rights summit in 2006; the first having taken place in Philadelphia, Mississippi, in 2005. The school board staff suggested to Ms. Glisson that the summit might be an appropriate time to undo a bit of McComb's racial past, by bringing back to McComb for the summit those students who had been expelled along with me in 1961 for participating in the walkout. The idea was that the students should be brought back and be given honorary diplomas to bring about a true reconciliation with our past. Finding close to one hundred former students, many of whom had migrated elsewhere, was a challenge, but many of the expelled students were located and invited.

It was Susan Glisson herself who reached out to me at my home in California. Our initial conversation was lengthy and emotion-filled, as I recounted to her many of my experiences of forty years before. I still had severely mixed emotions, because I had not, even at this time in my life, fully come to grips with all that had occurred when I was just sixteen and seventeen years old. Ms. Glisson's sincerity and sense of caring pervaded our initial conversation, and I began to feel that perhaps, just perhaps, this event in McComb would help me address once and for all the pain and heartbreak that had accompanied my courageous stand in 1961. We concluded our conversation by my expressing interest in participating in the event that was being planned for June 2006.

But just when I began to think that "reconciliation" was actually possible, the ghosts of my past reappeared, as menacing as they had been in 1961. While the initial concept was to offer honorary diplomas to all of the students who walked out, the school authorities unilaterally changed the plan, asserting that only those who would have graduated in 1962 should receive honorary diplomas. That number was small, only about fifteen, as most of the seniors in 1961–62 did not walk out with us. When this was related to me by Ms. Glisson, I felt that what was being done was deliberate, as the school authorities wanted to make sure that I did not receive any recognition. I was viewed, rightfully or wrongfully, as the leader of the walk-out. I was seething with anger as I could not believe that people, who were not even involved in the decisions forty years before, could be so heartless. But Ms. Glisson encouraged me to come to the summit, saying that the conference would at the very least be a first step toward coming to terms with the past.

My tormentors from the past were not through, however. When word began to spread that I had been invited to the summit and asked to be a speaker, the attorney who had represented the school board in 1961 approached the school superintendent and told him that I should not be allowed to participate in the event. He told the big racist lie that he and others, including the Sovereignty Commission, had spread about me—that I had not been expelled from school for my civil rights related activities, but rather I had been expelled because of promiscuity. That was, of course, a false, racist, and malicious accusation. The superintendent approached Ms. Glisson and told her what the former school board attorney had told him, and he asked her to contact me and ask me if the allegations were true. Much to Ms. Glisson's credit, she refused to do so, suggesting to Mr. Cooper that character assassinations such as the attorney was making about me were typical of what white supremacists had done in the 1960s. But Ms. Glisson's good efforts did not prevail.

Some members of the school board became uncomfortable and began to suggest that the summit be cancelled, as it was arousing great passions among the community and school board members. Former Governor Winter himself had to intervene, but even with his intervention, the issues surrounding the conference and my being involved would not go away. A few days before the conference was to take place, a school board official approached Ms. Glisson and told her that the charges and issues involving me had not been laid to rest, that the school system was very nervous about the whole event, and that I should be "uninvited" from speaking at the graduation ceremony.

Ms. Glisson set up a meeting with that school official, with Jackie Martin Byrd, and with the superintendent. The first item was the limitation of the issuance of the diplomas to the seniors in 1961–62. The school representatives would not back down on this. As to my attendance, the superintendent acquiesced to my attendance, but insisted that I not be allowed to speak. The superintendent took the position that anything that had happened to me in 1961 was a result of state action and not action by the school board. My classmate Jackie Martin Byrd spoke up on my behalf, telling the superintendent that the walk-out at the school was a direct result of my being expelled by the principal, upon orders from the school superintendent, and if I was not allowed to attend and speak, many of the former students would not attend, as they viewed me as their hero. Mr. Cooper finally broke the impasse by saying that I could attend and speak, but that I should be told that I would only be allowed to talk for five minutes.

Ms. Glisson called me while I was packing for my trip to Mississippi. She explained all that had taken place, including the fact that I would not be receiving a diploma at the event and that the school board was saying that it was the state, not the school board that had prompted my expulsion from school. I was incensed by the actions of the superintendent and the school board and thought for a moment that I should wash my hands of the affair, thank Ms. Glisson for all she had done, and stay and forget the whole thing. Ms. Glisson expressed her understanding, but the more I thought about what was taking place forty years after the initial insults I had received, my anger turned as it often does to determination. Determination not to let them win. Determination to make something positive of the entire situation by confronting my persecutors as I had done many years before.

Even after all these years it's difficult to explain exactly what was taken from me when I was jailed and exiled. People who hear or read my story know that my freedom was stolen, that my mother lost her job and was forced to leave McComb to find employment, that I was separated from my family, and that my education was halted. But how can you explain exactly how all this truly changed one's life. I'm not sure what my life would have been like had these events not happened to me; I don't know what I would have accomplished or how many more lives I might have impacted. What I do know is that a fear was instilled within me that continues until today. I know that I lost all trust in humankind. When I allow my mind to think back on those days, I'm engulfed in emotions and sometimes can't help crying. I know I was changed, and it was a change that was chosen for me by people who meant to do me harm. The saying is that "time heals all wounds," but the truth is that while we may be able to live through horrible experiences, the pain often revisits us, at times with great intensity.

I BOARDED THE PLANE for Mississippi, flying rather than taking the train which has always been my preferred method of travel. My emotions kept going back and forth and up and down, and as a severe diabetic I knew that this was not good for me. When I arrived in Mississippi, I immediately tried to get the sense of my family and community at large about the event and what was taking place related to me. What I learned further deepened my resolve. From trusted community members, I learned about Superintendent Cooper's plan to undo the consent decree. I was determined that this should not happen, as it would further damage the black students of McComb who were now virtually the only attendees of the local public schools. I worked on a plan. Wouldn't it be rich irony if forty years after the original walkout that I and the other students should walk out on this event, to protest anew the abject unfairness of what the school district was doing to us, the insult to the majority of us who were not receiving honorary diplomas, forty-plus years after we were expelled.

I met with Ms. Glisson on the first day of the conference. I was to receive the "Moral Compass" award from the Winter Institute that day, for my having stepped forward when hardly anyone else had done so, to become the conscience of my community. I told Ms. Glisson that I was considering a walkout of the next night's event, the graduation ceremony, as a protest against the continuing wrongdoing on the part of the school officials. I felt that she should be fully informed as I knew that she had worked very hard to have the event take place, and I did not want to undermine her well-motivated actions. Rather, I wanted the school board officials to understand that they could not continue to slap us in the face. While Ms. Glisson did not directly suggest that what I was doing was counterproductive, I could see the pain in her eyes as she indicated that a walkout might cause grave harm to the current McComb students, the children and grandchildren of those who walked out in 1961. Her measured response tugged at my heart strings because the last thing I ever wanted was to inflict on anyone else the kind of harm and hurt that I had encountered.

Later in the day, I was warmly received by all attendees of the conference when I was presented the Moral Compass award.

Afterwards, Jackie Martin Byrd approached me. She said Ms. Glisson had told her about my thinking about a walkout. Jackie knew me well and knew that once I had decided to do something, little could dissuade me. However, she echoed Ms. Glisson's sentiment that a walkout would inflame the situation rather promote future well-being. I heeded her and Ms. Glisson's words.

That evening was celebratory. Many of the former students who had walked out with me attended the events. We were older, grayer, and wrinkled but we shared many moments from the past, as former colleagues do at any reunion. I did not mention anything about my thoughts about a second walkout, but I did give a fiery speech and I did not limit myself to the five minutes that the superintendent wanted. I talked about the events of the past, of the pride I felt then and the pride I felt now on looking out at my friends who had the courage to walk out because I had been unfairly expelled from school for my civil rights activities. I told them that the courage they had exhibited then was equally important in today's world where so many have become complacent and did not bother to exercise their rights, including their right to vote for which many of us had suffered and some, including people in our own community, had died.

I then took on the superintendent directly. I urged those assembled to continue the fight and not allow the superintendent to undermine everything that we had fought for. The consent decree that was put in place in the 1970s must remain in place. It was the only thing that protected us, our children, and the children who attended the McComb public schools. To allow the superintendent and those acting in concert with him to discharge the consent decree would be a step backwards.

As I SPOKE, I noticed a white man smiling at me from the front row seats. I did not know him, and in light of all that had taken place, I was not sure that he did not mean ill will toward me—I knew that there were people in the white community who would rather harm me than listen to what I had to say. As I finished my presentation to a standing ovation (except the now red-faced superintendent), this gentleman approached me. He introduced himself as Dr. Randall O'Brien and said that he had something to give me. He told me his story. In 1961, he was attending a segregated white school in McComb. Coincidentally, he had a crush on a classmate who had the same name as mine, Brenda Travis. He was struck by our names being the same when he read in the McComb papers back in 1961 that I was put in jail. Over the years, after serving honorably in Vietnam and obtaining a PhD and becoming an educator in Texas, he still remembered my story. When in 2006 he read something about the event that was going to take place in our joint hometown and that I would be honored, it all came back to him and he resolved to attend.

As we stood there talking, he reached into his pocket and pulled out the Bronze Star that he had received for valor in Vietnam and handed it to me. He said that it was not him who deserved the Bronze Star, but rather it was me and all those who had fought for the rights of others here in the Deep South of the USA who deserved to be honored.

He said to me: "Some people are asked to fight for their country. But no one should ever be asked to fight her country and that is exactly what you had to do."

He pinned his Bronze Star on me and we both cried and hugged. Out of an evening that had been fraught with difficulty and emotion, this singular act by a courageous man was the highlight of everything that had occurred. In many ways it symbolized everything that I had fought for. A white man of courage had recognized a black woman of courage by giving her a prized possession. I was truly honored, and that Bronze Star is one of the most treasured awards that I have received over the years. Needless to say, Dr. O'Brien and I remain friends to this day, sharing this common bond.

WHILE I DID NOT receive my "honorary diploma" in 2006, and I am told that my presentation enraged the then-superintendent, a change did occur five years later. 2011 marked the fiftieth anniversary of my expulsion and the student walkout. In response, Lisa Deer, a community outreach director working for Teaching for Change, began a program in the McComb schools working with public school students. The participating students researched the history of civil rights activities in McComb and resolved to set up a commemorative event, including workshops, discussions, and a driving tour of McComb, to celebrate the Burglund High School Walkout. I was invited to attend along with many other civil rights veterans and my fellow 1961 students who walked out with me, including Ann Harris, Carol Jean Hughes, Joe Lewis, and Earnestine Ridley Weatherspoon.

The commemorative events took place at the old Burglund High School. The building now houses a middle school and, amazingly enough, is named after the black collaborator, Commodore Dewey Higgins, who expelled me from Burglund. You can imagine how difficult it was for me to walk in the doors of that school, for only the second time in fifty years, to see that the school board had named it after the man who had betrayed me and my fellow walkout students and the whole black community of McComb.

When I walked into the building in 2011, I was flooded with memories. Some were of good times with my brother, good times with friends. But most of all, I could see Principal Higgins's contorted face as he told me that I could no longer attend the school—all because I had the courage that he did not have to stand up to the system. As I floated through the memories, I heard my name called. The present superintendent of the McComb schools,

Therese Palmertree, and the president of the McComb School Board of Trustees, Bettye Nunnery—a white woman and a black woman—asked me to step forward. They then presented what I had been deprived of many years ago and what I had to go into exile to obtain, an honorary diploma from the McComb school district.

I awoke from my reverie and was overwhelmed and cried.

ONE OF THE OBVIOUS changes for the worse in McComb, in Mississippi generally, and throughout the South is a sad legacy of *Brown v. Board of Education* which is seldom talked or written about. I am referring to the re-segregation of the public schools. Integration came to the McComb schools in 1965 with the initial pioneering efforts of my sister, Marionette Travis, my cousin, Bernice Belton, and a few of their friends. In the 1970s, the court-ordered consent decree brought about full integration of the public schools. However, the schools did not stay integrated for long. One of the ugly, well-kept secrets in this country is that once the schools became integrated, almost all of the white students left the public schools to go to private academies which sprang up overnight. Most of these are justifiably tagged with the label of "seg academies." Many were set up with government assistance and often with public funds.

In McComb, for instance, Parklane Academy* was created in 1970 as a "private Christian school" for grades K4–12. I am told that the first black student "integrated" this bastion of segregated bliss in the 2013–14 school year.

The creation of Parklane and its segregated success over the years has harmed the community greatly. Since the white parents are paying tuition at this private school, sometimes subsidized, there is no incentive for them to support the McComb public schools in any

* It has a famous alumna—the pop singer Britney Spears.

way. Needed school tax increases are routinely defeated, and the public school facilities and programs deteriorate while the Parklane students enjoy the same benefit that their parents and grandparents had fifty years before—separate and unequal education.

The community as a whole has suffered. McComb became a majority black community as whites (and some middle-class blacks) moved outside the city while rural African Americans moved into it. In addition, because of McComb's proximity to New Orleans, there was an influx of poverty-stricken residents who were relocated because of Hurricane Katrina in 2005.

What has this done to the community? For the most part, there is no community. While in my youth my family and our neighbors were as poor as many of the residents are today, we did have a sense of community. We shared what little we had, our produce, our water, whatever resources we had. But it was more than just a physical sharing; there was a unique bond between us. While we were the Travis family, proud and poor, we were part of a community where our parents were each and every adult member of the community with whom we came into contact. Neighbors could scold us and bring us into line, and any of us would reach out to help others who were even less well-heeled than we were. This sense of community no longer exists in McComb.

Traveling through McComb today is like traveling through a larger Mississippi city like Jackson or even a northern city like Detroit. One of the first things one sees is "burglar bars" on the windows of virtually every home. Abandoned homes blight the neighborhoods. Drugs and alcohol are prolific. As in many communities, young black men in McComb are more likely to be in prison than in college. If a neighbor, or a teacher, for that matter, were to reach out to "instruct" a youth regarding his or her behavior, that neighbor or teacher would likely be challenged by the child or a parent. Even more sadly, many black residents, especially the young adults, do not even "bother" to vote, as they do not see how they have a stake in what is going on in the community, the state or the nation. The fact that "we the people," as my friend Bob Moses is wont to say, elected a black man president and even reelected him does not resonate with the youth in McComb. If a student at McComb High School were asked to identify C. C. Bryant or Brenda Travis, most would shrug their shoulders. They could say these were people for whom streets were named, but they would know little or nothing of Mr. Bryant's or my own sacrifices.

Within this educational and spiritual void, I knew it was time for me to muster my courage again and take action fifty-two years after my first courageous steps. In 2013, I founded the Brenda Travis Foundation for Historical Education in my hometown of McComb. Although I have incredible strength of purpose, I do not have great material resources. But I wanted to create a place where young people could learn about their past, our past, in a safe environment full of books and materials related to the civil rights movement generally, and McComb's place in that civil rights movement specifically. I think it is essential that the people of our community know and understand their history and the important sacrifices that C. C. Bryant, Webb Owens, and others made toward bringing equal justice to our community. McComb and its black citizenry played an important role in the civil rights movement and that role should not be forgotten but rather built upon. I have opened a center which is designed for education outreach to offer children and adults of all ages a place to interact and learn and create a better community—better than what it was when I came up, and certainly better than what it is today.

MARTIN LUTHER KING JR. and my SNCC brothers and sisters always talked about the "beloved community" that they hoped to create. While that vision has not been realized, in the years that I have left I will work in my community to help inspire the youth of today. Perhaps, just perhaps, another sixteen-year-old will come along to risk all to bring about change in the spirit of what I tried to do more than fifty years ago. Our work continues . . .

A Bronze Star for Brenda

J. RANDALL O'BRIEN[*]

C ivil rights heroes and heroines number in the hundreds, nay thousands, tens of thousands, from the 1960s alone. Immortalized in the pages of American history, many of our country's bravest soldiers earned their medals of valor on battlefields of strange name: lunch counters, bus stations, courthouses, public schools, jails. Purple Hearts rained upon crowded jail cells and bare black backs in darkened forests where Satan's army tortured God's precious children of color. There hooded hoodlums and Klansmen cops dispensed pain to prophets, wounds to warriors, evil to any who courageously worked for racial equality.

Jesus was an African American in the 1960s. Anti-Christ Christians and other hate-filled infidels killed him—again. And again, and again and again.

Wasn't that a crucifixion on the balcony of the Lorraine Hotel in Memphis in 1968? Didn't Chaney, Schwerner, and Goodman precede Dr. King on Golgotha in Philadelphia, Mississippi, in 1964? Wasn't Medgar Evers nailed at Calvary by a bullet to the back in Jackson in 1963? And what about the nearly anonymous Amite County farmer-messiah, Herbert Lee? What happened to him in

---

[*] President, Carson-Newman University, Jefferson City, Tennessee.

September of '61? All of these are heroes, fallen heroes, national heroes, and heroes of mine.

There are thousands more. One, a young African American girl, from McComb, Mississippi, stands out.

On Saturday, August 26, 1961, African American Mississippians Hollis Watkins and Curtis (Elmer) Hayes sat-in at Woolworth's "Whites Only" lunch counter in my hometown of McComb, thereby becoming two of the first persons to take direct action against segregation in the state. For their revolutionary bravery they were promptly arrested, jailed for thirty days, and charged with breach of peace.

Four days later, on Wednesday, August 30, 1961, Robert Talbert, Isaac Lewis, and sixteen-year-old Brenda Travis sat-in at the segregated Greyhound bus station in McComb. They, too, were arrested immediately and incarcerated for twenty-eight days in the county jail.

After their release from jail, Ike and Brenda were expelled from Burglund High, McComb's high school for African Americans, refused readmission, and therefore handed, in effect, lifetime sentences of punishing poverty. Southern blacks in that era, even with high school educations, could not, as a rule, expect to earn a fair, living wage. But to be denied the opportunity to earn even a high school diploma represented cruel and unusual punishment, a sentence of raw poverty for life.

On October 4, 1961, approximately one hundred and twenty of Brenda and Ike's classmates angrily protested the expulsions and oppressive culture of racial discrimination by marching from Burglund High School through town. Singing "We Shall Overcome," they were led by young Brenda to the steps of City Hall. One-by-one the students ascended the steps to kneel and pray. There they were beaten and kicked by cops and other fine Christian citizens, then arrested.

Brenda related years later, "I believe I was predestined to become an activist. I joined the NAACP and became involved in the movement to get people to vote. But they were afraid."

Jailed again, this time for her role in the student march, Brenda and the other students sang and prayed through the night. After several days, Brenda related, "They took me out of jail. Said, 'We're taking you to Jackson to see your attorney.' After a long drive they pulled the car up to the gates of the Reform School in Oakley. My family, nobody knew where I was. My family suffered."

Though sentenced to a year in reformatory school, the young teenager was released before completing her full term under one condition established by the governor: she must leave the state within twenty-four hours of her release!

Following years of exile, Brenda returned to Mississippi on June 21, 2006, for the forty-fifth anniversary of the 1961 direct action against segregation in Mississippi. Determined, I got in my automobile, pulled out of my driveway, and drove ten hours from my home in Texas to find Brenda in McComb. I had something to say to her. I had something to give her.

Following two days of recognitions, speeches, awards ceremonies, a moving graduation exercise nearly a half-century too late for the expelled seniors of the Burglund High Class of '62, and a final stirring address to a full house by Brenda Travis, the right moment arrived for me to approach Brenda. My heart raced.

"Brenda," I began, "I'm Randall O'Brien. I'm a minister and the executive vice president and provost of Baylor University. I grew up in McComb."

"Oh, I'm very glad to meet you," she replied.

"No, the honor is all mine. You are a hero of mine. I was twelve years old when you sat-in at the bus station and marched on City Hall. You were sixteen. Those remain, for me, two of the greatest acts of bravery in my lifetime."

"How very kind of you. Thank you, Randall."

I continued, "Brenda, what happened to you was one of the darkest travesties of justice in American history. I am ashamed; I am embarrassed; I am angry. I am also changed by you, by your life, your courage, your cries for justice. As you know, our lives always travel down paths of continuation or compensation in the area of racial injustice, one or the other. Your witness, and the courageous work of your sisters and brothers, has been a huge influence upon my life. I've tried to live my life to help compensate for all the wrong done to African Americans. How can I say 'Thank you,' Brenda, for who you are and for who you've helped me to become?"

Brenda tried to speak, but couldn't. Her eyes filled with tears. We hugged. Slipping my right hand into my pants pocket, I clutched the gift I had brought for her, pulled it out, and placed it in Brenda's hand.

Leaning back from our embrace while looking into my heroine's eyes, still holding her hand, I whispered, "A few years after your civil rights battles for our country, I fought for our country on a different battlefield—in Vietnam. Sometimes in an imperfect world a person might need to fight for his country. But no one—no one—should ever have to fight her country!"

Nodding humbly in silent agreement, brown eyes swimming in tears, Brenda stood still, we both did, planted on holy ground.

"For my service in Vietnam I was awarded the Bronze Star," I said. "For your gallantry, Brenda, you were awarded reform school and cruel exile from your home state and family. You were so many times more heroic than I ever was! I want you to have my Bronze Star, Brenda, for your heroism. You already have my admiration and my heart."

Weeping, plunging us into tearful embrace again, Brenda whispered to me through her sobs, "I don't know what to say."

"You don't have to say anything. I thought about saving my

medals for my children, maybe giving my bronze star to my son, so my children would have something to remember me by. Then I thought, no, this is how I want to be remembered: Brenda Travis gave her youth for civil rights for all Americans; Daddy gave his Bronze Star to Brenda Travis."

Brenda Travis: Real American Hero!

For Further Reading

Adickes, Sandra E. *The Legacy of a Freedom School*. New York: Palgrave Macmillan (2005).

Armstrong, Thomas M. and Natalie R. Bell. *Autobiography of a Freedom Rider*. Deerfield Beach, Illinois: Health Communications, Inc., 2011.

Arsenault, Raymond. *Freedom Riders*. New York: Oxford University Press, 2006.

Beito, David T. and Linda Royster Beito. *Black Maverick*. Urbana: University of Illinois Press, 2009.

Billings, David. *Deep Denial*. Roselle, New Jersey: Crandall, Dostie & Douglass Books, Inc., 2016.

Boyett, Patricia Michelle. *Right to Revolt*. Jackson: University Press of Mississippi (2015).

Branch, Taylor. *Parting the Waters America in the King Years*. New York: Simon and Schuster, 1988.

_____, *Pillar of Fire*. New York: Simon & Schuster, 1998.

Bruner, Eric. *And Gently He Shall Lead Them: Robert Parris Moses and Civil Rights in Mississippi*. New York: New York University Press, 1994.

Cagin, Seth and Philip Dray. *We Are Not Afraid*. New York: Macmillan, 1988.

Cantarow, Ellen with Susan Gushee O'Malley and Sharon Hartman Strom. *Moving the Mountain: Women Working for Social Change*. New York: The Feminist Press, 1980.

Cobb, Jr., Charles E. *This Nonviolent Stuff'll Get You Killed*. New York: Basic Books, 2014.

Collier-Thomas, Bettye and V.P. Franklin. *My Soul is a Witness*. New York: Henry Holt, 1999.

Dittmer, John. *Local People: The Struggle for Civil Rights in Mississippi*. Urbana: University of Illinois Press, 1994.

Erenrich, Susie, ed. *Freedom is a Constant Struggle*. Montgomery: Black Belt Press, 2010.

Forman, James. *The Making of Black Revolutionaries: A Personal Account*. New York: Macmillan, 1972.

Geiger, Roger L., ed. *History of Higher Education Annual 2003-2004*, Vol. 23. New Brunswick, New Jersey: Transaction Publishers, 2005.

Haas, Jeffrey. *The Assassination of Fred Hampton*. Chicago: Lawrence Hill, 2010.

Halberstam, David. *The Children*. New York: Random House, 1998.

Hayden, Tom. *Reunion*. New York: Random House, 1988.

Hill, Lance. *The Deacons for Defense*. Chapel Hill: The University of North Carolina Press, 2004.

Holsaert, Faith, et al., eds. *Hands on the Freedom Plow*. Urbana: University of Illinois Press, 2010.

Houck, David W. and David E. Dixon, eds. *Women and the Civil Rights Movement, 1954-1965*. Mississippi: The University Press of Mississippi, 2009.

King, Rev. Ed and Trent Watts. *Ed King's Mississippi*. Jackson: The University Press of Mississippi, 2014.

Lewis, Anthony and The New York Times. *Portrait of a Decade: The Second American Revolution; A First Hand Account of the Struggle for Civil Rights, 1954-1964*. New York: Random House, 1964.

Lewis, John with Michael D'Orso. *Walking with the Wind*. New York: Simon and Schuster, 1998.

Marshall, James P. *Student Activism and Civil Rights in Mississippi*. Baton Rouge: Louisiana State University Press, 2013.

McClymer, John F. Mississippi Freedom Summer. Toronto: Wadsworth/Thompson, 2004.

Moody, Anne. *Coming of Age in Mississippi*. New York: The Dial Press, 1968.

Moses, Robert P. and Charles E. Cobb, Jr. *Radical Equations*. Boston: Beacon Press, 2001.

Olson, Lynne. *Freedom's Daughters: The Unsung Heroines of the Civil Rights From 1830 to 1970*. New York: Scribner, 2001.

Payne, Charles M. *I've Got the Light of Freedom: The Organizing Tradition and the Mississippi Freedom Struggle*. Berkeley: University of California Press, 1995.

Raines, Howell. *My Soul Is Rested*. New York: G. O. Putnam's Sons, 1977.

Ransby, Barbara. *Ella Baker and the Black Freedom Movement: A Radical*

Democratic Vision. Chapel Hill: University of North Carolina Press, 2003.

Silver, James W. *Mississippi: The Closed Society.* New York: Harcourt Brace & World Inc., 1963.

Tucker, Shirley. *Mississippi from Within.* New York: Arco Publishing Co., 1965.

Tyson, Timothy B. *The Blood of Emmett Till.* New York: Simon & Schuster, 2017.

Walls LaNier, Carlotta with Lisa Frazier Page. *A Mighty Long Way.* New York: One World Books, 2009.

Wand, Jason Morgan. *Hanging Bridge.* New York: Oxford University Press, 2016.

Ward, Geoff K. *The Black Child-Savers: Racial Democracy and Juvenile Justice.* Chicago: The University of Chicago Press, 2012.

Watkins, Hollis with C. Leigh McInnis. *Brother Hollis: The Sankofa of a Movement Man.* Clinton, MS: Sankofa Southern Publishing, 2015.

Williams, Jakobi. *From the Bullet to the Ballot.* Chapel Hill: University of North Carolina Press, 2013.

Wright, Simeon and Herb Boyd. *Simeon's Story.* Chicago: Lawrence Hill Books, 2010.

Zellner, Bob with Constance Curry. *The Wrong Side of Murder Creek.* Montgomery: NewSouth Books, 2008.

Zinn, Howard. *SNCC: The New Abolitionists.* 2d. Ed. Boston: Beacon Press, 1968.

Index